W9-AUX-497

healthy heart
cookbook

WITHDRAWN

healthy heart cookbook

OVER 50 SIMPLE, TASTY AND
NUTRITIOUS RECIPES THAT ARE LOW IN
SALT, FAT AND CHOLESTEROL

HELEN MIDDLETON

LORENZ BOOKS

Mount Laurel Library
100 Walt Whitman Avenue
Mount Laurel, NJ 08054-9539
856-234-7319
www.mtlaurel.lib.nj.us

This edition is published by Lorenz Books

Lorenz Books is an imprint of Anness Publishing Ltd
Hermes House, 88–89 Blackfriars Road, London SE1 8HA
tel. 020 7401 2077; fax 020 7633 9499
www.lorenzbooks.com; info@anness.com

© Anness Publishing Limited 1999, 2003

UK agent: The Manning Partnership Ltd, 6 The Old Dairy, Melcombe Road, Bath BA2 3LR
tel. 01225 478444; fax 01225 478440; sales@manning-partnership.co.uk

UK distributor: Grantham Book Services Ltd, Isaac Newton Way, Alma Park Industrial Estate, Grantham, Lincs NG31 9SD
tel. 01476 541080; fax 01476 541061; orders@gbs.tbs-ltd.co.uk

North American agent/distributor: National Book Network, 4501 Forbes Boulevard, Suite 200, Lanham, MD 20706
tel. 301 459 3366; fax 301 429 5746; www.nbnbooks.com

Australian agent/distributor: Pan Macmillan Australia, Level 18, St Martins Tower, 31 Market St, Sydney, NSW 2000
tel. 1300 135 113; fax 1300 135 103; customer.service@macmillan.com.au

New Zealand agent/distributor: David Bateman Ltd, 30 Tarndale Grove, Off Bush Road, Albany, Auckland
tel. (09) 415 7664; fax (09) 415 8892

All rights reserved. No part of this publication may be reproduced, stored in a retrieval system, or transmitted in any way or by
any means, electronic, mechanical, photocopying, recording or otherwise, without the prior written permission of the copyright holder.

A CIP catalogue record for this book is available from the British Library.

Publisher: Joanna Lorenz
Senior Cookery Editor: Linda Fraser
Project Editor: Doreen Palamartschuk
Designer: Ian Sandom
Photographers: James Duncan, Michelle Garrett, Amanda Heywood,
David Jordan, Don Last, William Lingwood and Peter Reilly
Stylists: Madeleine Brehaut, Jo Harris, Clare Louise Hunt,
Fiona Tillett and Judy Williams
Recipes: Catherine Atkinson, Christine France, Carole Handslip, Sue Maggs, Kathy Man, Annie Nichols,
Anne Sheasby and Liz Trigg
Production Controller: Joanna King

Previously published in the *Healthy Eating Library* series.

1 3 5 7 9 10 8 6 4 2

NOTES
For all recipes, quantities are given in both metric and imperial measures and, where appropriate, measures are also given in
standard cups and spoons. Follow one set, but not a mixture, because they are not interchangeable.
Standard spoon and cup measures are level.
1 tsp = 5ml, 1 tbsp = 15ml, 1 cup = 250ml/8fl oz
Australian standard tablespoons are 20ml. Australian readers should use 3 tsp in place of 1 tbsp for measuring small
quantities of gelatine, cornflour, salt, etc.
Medium eggs are used unless otherwise stated.

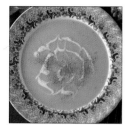

CONTENTS

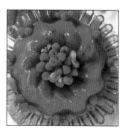

INTRODUCTION

Making simple changes to our diet and to our lifestyle can help us reduce the risk of coronary heart disease (CHD). There are three main things we can do to improve our way of life: we can become more active – take 30 minutes moderate exercise five times a week; we can give up smoking – see your general practitioner or call one of the numerous helplines for advice; and we can learn to cope with stress. If we also improve our diet, we will enhance these changes and in addition will help to control the other major risk factors of CHD, which are: raised blood cholesterol, raised blood pressure and obesity (or being overweight).

Eating for a healthy heart isn't difficult. As a first step, we should eat at least five portions of vegetables and/or fruit a day, and make sure that at least half our meals consist of starchy carbo-hydrate foods like bread, pasta, rice and potatoes, without too much added fat. Even simple changes to eating habits can make a considerable difference. Cooking our own food puts us in control and makes it easy to limit the amount of fat (particularly saturated fat), salt and sugar we consume. The recipes in this book prove just how delicious a well-balanced diet can be, and there are numerous techniques and suggestions for eliminating the less desirable elements in our food while retaining – and even enhancing – the flavour. So, change to a healthier lifestyle and follow the food recommendations in this book, then relax and enjoy life – it'll do your heart good.

To maintain a healthy diet you should eat at least five portions of fruit or vegetables daily.

EATING A HEALTHY DIET

Eat a good variety of different foods every day to make sure you get all the nutrients you need.

- Skimmed milk contains the same amount of calcium, protein and B vitamins as whole milk, but a fraction of the fat.
- Natural low-fat yogurt, cottage cheese and fromage frais are all high in calcium and protein, and are good substitutes for cream.
- Starchy foods such as rice, bread, potatoes, cereals, pulses and pasta should be eaten at every meal. These foods provide energy and some vitamins, minerals and dietary fibre.
- Vegetables, salads and fruits should form a major part of the diet, about 450g/1lb should be eaten each day.
- Eat meat in moderation but eat plenty of fish, particularly oily fish such as trout, mackerel, salmon, tuna, herring and sardines.

A few simple changes to a normal diet can reduce fat intake considerably.

The following tips and suggestions are designed to make the change to a healthier diet as easy as possible.

MEAT AND POULTRY

Red meats such as lamb, pork and beef are high in saturated fats, but chicken and turkey contain far less fat. Remove the skin before cooking and trim off any visible fat. Avoid sausages, burgers, pâtés, bacon and minced beef. Buy lean cuts of meat and skim any fat from the surface of stocks and stews.

DAIRY PRODUCTS

Replace whole milk with skimmed or semi-skimmed milk and use low-fat yogurt, low-fat crème fraîche or fromage frais instead of cream. Eat cream, cream cheese and hard cheese in moderation. There are reduced-fat cheeses on the market with 14 per cent fat content which is half the fat content of full-fat cheese. Use these wherever possible.

SPREADS, OILS AND DRESSINGS

Use butter, margarine and low-fat spreads sparingly. Try to avoid using fat and oil for cooking. If you have to use oil, choose olive, corn, sunflower, soya, rapeseed and peanut oils, which are low in saturates. Look out for oil-free dressings and reduced-fat mayonnaise.

HIDDEN FATS

Biscuits, cakes, pastries, snacks, processed meals and curries all contain high proportions of fat. Get into the habit of reading food labels carefully and looking for a low-fat option.

COOKING METHODS

Grill, poach and steam foods whenever possible. If you do fry foods, use as little fat as possible and pat off the excess after browning, with kitchen paper. Make sauces and stews by first cooking the onions and garlic in a small quantity of stock, rather than frying in oil.

Choose a variety of foods from the main food groups to ensure you have all the nutrients your body needs.

EATING LESS SALT

One of the steps we can take to reduce our risk of coronary heart disease is to cut down on the amount of salt we eat. Excessive salt intake can be linked to high blood pressure and is one of the main reasons why blood pressure tends to rise as we get older. (Other risk factors include low potassium intake and being overweight.)

Salt, together with potassium, is essential for a variety of bodily functions, but we tend to have far too much of it, largely through our consumption of processed foods. Canned, pre-packaged or "convenience" foods, takeaways and ready-prepared meals, contribute as much as 80 per cent of the salt in our diet, so preparing and cooking more of our own food is an excellent way of reducing our daily intake to the recommended 6 grammes.

Eating more non-processed foods – such as fresh vegetables, fruit, fish and meat – will have an added bonus in boosting our potassium levels.

Although cutting down on the amount of salt used during cooking and at the table is not enough on its own, it is a valuable step in helping to re-educate our tastebuds. The more salt we have, the more we want.

Gradually reduce the amount added to your food and what used to taste delicious soon seems excessively salty.

It's also a good idea to note which foods are high in salt and keep a check on how many of these we eat.

CUTTING DOWN
We often add salt out of habit; the following are some tips to help you cut down:

- Taste food before you shake on salt – and then use it only sparingly.
- Block up some of the holes in the salt cellar.
- Better still, do not add any kind of salt, including most salt substitutes, to your food, either when cooking or to the finished dish at the table.
- Replace salt in recipes with herbs and spices, garlic and lemon juice, mustard or chilli powder. A small quantity of wine or beer can also be added for extra flavour.
- Use fresh or frozen vegetables instead of canned.
- Chinese food in particular tends to be high in monosodium glutamate and salt, so enjoy it as an occasional treat, or make your own.
- Cook with a stock made from celery, onion, carrot and bouquet garni instead of stock cubes.
- Swap to lower-salt breads. Most bread contains two per cent salt, but read the labels. "Healthy eating" brands of bread can contain as little as 0.8 per cent salt and some health food stores sell bread baked with no added salt.

LOW-SALT VEGETABLE STOCK
This is an excellent way of making good use of any left-over vegetables and will produce a healthy, full-flavoured stock.

INGREDIENTS

Makes 1.75 litres/3 pints/7½ cups
1 onion
2 carrots
2 large celery sticks, plus any small amounts from the following: leek, celeriac, parsnip, turnip, courgette, cabbage or cauliflower trimmings, mushroom peelings
30ml/2 tbsp vegetable oil
bouquet garni
6 black peppercorns

2 Heat the oil in a large pan and fry the vegetables until soft and lightly browned. Add the remaining ingredients and cover with 1.75 litres/3 pints/7½ cups water.

3 Bring to the boil, skim the surface then partially cover and simmer for 1½ hours. Strain the stock and allow to cool. Store in a covered container in the refrigerator for 2–3 days.

1 Peel the onion and then quarter it. Chop all the vegetables into large pieces.

EATING LESS FAT

Another essential factor in the healthy diet is to reduce the amount of fat we eat, particularly the amount of saturated fat. This lowers our blood cholesterol levels, which, in turn, reduces the risk of CHD. At the moment 15–16 per cent of the calories we eat are from saturated fat. It is recommended that this is reduced to no more than ten per cent.

WHERE DO SATURATED FATS COME FROM?

As a general rule, saturated fats are solid at room temperature. The list includes lard, butter, hard cheese and the visible fat on meat. Saturated fats can also be "hidden" in products such as pork pies, cakes, biscuits, ice cream, pastry and chocolate. The major sources of saturated fats are full-fat dairy products (milk, cheese, cream), followed by fatty meat products (pies, pasties, sausages).

HOW MUCH FAT?

It is not a good idea to eliminate fat from our diet entirely. Limited amounts of some fats are essential for good health. The ideal is no more than three portions of fat per day. A portion equals:
• 5ml/1 tsp butter, margarine or cooking oil
• 10ml/2 tsp low-fat spread
• 5ml/1 tsp salad dressing or mayonnaise.

It is preferable to choose polyunsaturated fats, such as those found in vegetable oils, spreads or margarines labelled as being high in polyunsaturates, and oily fish.

Meat is a valuable source of protein, iron, B vitamins and minerals, while dairy foods contribute calcium, protein, B vitamins and vitamins A and D. To continue to benefit from these important nutrients, choose lean meat and low-fat dairy products where possible and eat in moderation. Most of us will come to no harm if we eat the occasional high-fat food, but as a general rule, it is wise to be wary of cream, cream-based desserts, chocolate, pastries, cakes, biscuits, ice cream, confectionery, crisps, rich sauces and gravies, fatty bacon, sausages and other meat products.

LOW-FAT SWAPS

Make low-fat substitutes wherever possible, such as:
• Skimmed or semi-skimmed milk for full-fat milk

• low-fat yogurt for full-fat varieties
• small amounts of lean meat for fatty meat products, e.g. sausages, sausage rolls, pâtés, luncheon meats, meat pies and pasties
• swap two meat meals a week with fish, especially oily fish (such as sardines, pilchards, herring, mackerel and salmon), which provide "omega 3" fatty acids. These fatty acids help to reduce blood viscosity, making it less likely to clot.

Eat a variety of white and oily fish, such as tuna, plaice, salmon, trout and mackerel.

HIGH-FIBRE FOODS

People who eat a diet rich in fibre tend to have lower blood cholesterol levels and are at a lower risk of CHD than those whose diet consists largely of refined foods. High fibre foods are also filling, which can be an asset when it comes to weight control. There are many types of fibre, but one in particular, soluble fibre, seems to be beneficial in binding cholesterol and preventing it from being deposited in the arteries.

SOURCES OF FIBRE

Foods high in soluble fibre include oats; beans and peas; apples and oranges; and green leafy vegetables, such as cabbage and spinach. To be effective sources of fibre, these vegetables need to be cooked and eaten without additional fats, so do not fry them or smother vegetables with butter or fatty sauces.

The best high fibre foods are those in which the fibre occurs naturally, such as cereals, vegetables and fruit. These foods are also rich in the protective antioxidant vitamin beta-carotene, vitamins C and E and the minerals zinc, selenium, manganese and copper. Antioxidants are substances that delay or prevent oxidation, which is the process by which oxygen combines with other substances. A by-product of oxidation is the production of free radicals. Free radicals in a living organism can be extremely harmful.

One of their effects is to damage artery walls, allowing cholesterol to be deposited and thus increasing the risk of heart disease. We cannot avoid encountering free radicals because we breathe oxygen and pollutants, such as cigarette smoke and chemicals, but we can limit their effect.

EATING MORE FIBRE

The easiest way to boost your fibre intake is to:
• Eat plenty of bread, pasta, rice and potatoes. Choose wholemeal bread and pasta, and brown rice

• Instead of buying biscuits and cakes, which can be high in sugar, salt and fats, bake wholemeal scones, muffins or buns. Serve them plain or with a mere scraping of low-fat spread
• Enjoy plenty of breakfast cereal (with low-fat milk and no sugar) but choose wholegrain varieties with little or no added sugar, such as shredded wheat, puffed wheat, porridge oats and muesli. Avoid sugar-coated cereals
• Use more pulses (beans, peas, lentils, split peas) either alone or to replace some of the meat in dishes like cottage pie, shepherd's pie, curry,

pasta sauces or chilli con carne. Make frequent use of canned beans, including baked beans
• Eat at least five portions of vegetables and/or fruit every day.

AVOID BRAN

Bran added to refined food is not as good for you as starchy foods, vegetables and fruits. Too much raw bran can bind minerals, making them unavailable to the body. Bran may conquer constipation, but it does not share the cholesterol-lowering effect of other fibres that are found in starchy foods, fresh vegetables and fruits.

Bread, pasta, rice and muesli are all good sources of fibre.

CHOLESTEROL

Cholesterol is a waxy substance that occurs naturally in the body, when it is referred to as blood cholesterol. It is also present in foods of animal origin (dietary cholesterol). The higher the level of cholesterol in the blood, the greater our risk of heart disease. Some cholesterol is essential for functions such as the making of cell membranes, and the body usually maintains a balance, making more if needed. However, if the blood contains too much cholesterol, this can cause many problems.

GOOD AND BAD CHOLESTEROL

There are two main types of blood cholesterol. The "good" type is high density lipoprotein (HDL), which carries excess cholesterol to the liver for removal from the body. The "bad" type is low density lipoprotein (LDL), which deposits cholesterol on the artery walls. Adequate amounts of HDL lower the risk of coronary heart disease, but excessive amounts of LDL raise the risk.

At one time, it was thought that cholesterol-rich foods were largely responsible for high blood cholesterol levels, but it is now known that the amount of cholesterol we eat is not as significant as our intake of fats. Saturated fats are, once again, the villains of the piece, leading to increased levels of LDL.

WHERE IS CHOLESTEROL FOUND?

Although the link between dietary cholesterol and blood cholesterol is disputed, it can be useful to know which foods are cholesterol-rich. Dietary cholesterol is found only in animal foods: the richest sources are liver, shellfish and eggs. The general advice is to eat no more than four eggs a week. If you like mussels, prawns, shrimps and other shellfish (which, although high in cholesterol, are low in fat), eat them in moderation. Grill,

barbecue or cook shellfish in paella and risotto. Serve them, Asian-style in thin broth, but not in creamy French seafood dishes.

High levels of cholesterol are also found in fatty meat, high-fat cheeses and full-fat milk, but as we have seen, eating for a healthy heart limits these foods anyway. They do not have to be given up completely, just eaten in sensible proportions.

READ THE LABELS

Nutritional labels state how much fat a food contains. Some even state what percentage is saturated but very few

Make plenty of salads and cooked vegetable dishes and avoid adding too much fat to your diet.

labels give information on cholesterol. If there is no statistical data on the label, ingredients are listed in descending order by weight. Common names for saturated fat on food labels include hydrogenated vegetable oil or fat; palm oil; coconut oil; cocoa butter; shortening (solid vegetable fat); animal fat; milk solids and non-milk fat. If any of these names appears high up the list of ingredients, the food is likely to be high in saturated fat.

LIFE IS FOR LIVING

People who exercise regularly have lower levels of coronary heart disease, and those with CHD who exercise are less likely to die as a result of the disease. Most people need to take more exercise but how much is enough? Taking positive action to stop smoking and to lower your stress levels is also an excellent way of getting a healthier lifestyle, while alcohol needs to be treated with caution.

HOW MUCH PHYSICAL ACTIVITY SHOULD YOU DO?

Until recently 20 minutes of vigorous aerobic exercise three times a week was the prescription for preventing CHD. New research, however, shows that even moderate amounts of less intense exercise can be beneficial. Because many people are so sedentary, even getting out of the chair and taking some exercise for half an hour, once or twice a week, can have a positive effect. Regular exercise – about 30 minutes of moderate intensity for five days out of seven – has substantial benefits. Exercise of moderate intensity makes you breathe slightly harder. Your heart rate will be slightly raised, so you will feel warmer, but you will not be out of breath.

MODERATE INTENSITY ACTIVITY

Aerobic capacity varies between individuals, but examples of moderate intensity activity include brisk walking (6–7 kph/4 mph); heavy do-it-yourself work in the home; gardening (such as raking leaves or using a power mower); washing the car; doing strenuous housework and lifting or carrying heavy loads. Golf, table tennis, social dancing and keep-fit (all at an intensity that makes you breathe hard and sweat a little) are also worthwhile, as are slow stair climbing, cycling at more than 16 kph/10 mph, gentle swimming, playing doubles tennis and doing low-intensity aerobic exercises.

SMOKING

Many doctors consider smoking to be the biggest risk factor when it comes to CHD, with the risk increasing relative to the number of years someone has smoked and how many cigarettes have been smoked.
The harmful effects are linked to carbon monoxide in the smoke (which decreases the amount of oxygen to the heart) and nicotine (which makes the heart work harder). In a person with CHD this may lead to disturbances in heart rhythm. Both nicotine and carbon monoxide increase the tendency for blood to clot. Free radicals in smoke also increase damage to the artery walls, making it easier for cholesterol to be deposited.

STRESS

Despite the popular view that top grade executives with high levels of responsibility are most likely to suffer stress, current research suggests that it is often the lower grade workers whose jobs make high demands but who have low control over their work (and lives) who suffer more CHD. Research continues into stress and heart disease. Meanwhile it seems that good relaxation techniques, job satisfaction and leisure-time physical activity help us to cope with stress and probably reduce the risk of CHD.

ALCOHOL

Light and moderate drinkers appear to have a lower death rate from CHD than either non-drinkers or heavy drinkers. Light to moderate means 1–3 units a day, or not more than 21 per week for women/28 for men; possibly up to 28 a week for post-menopausal women. Protection may be the result of alcohol raising levels of HDL cholesterol in the blood. Another factor may be the antioxidant properties of some drinks, mainly red wine. If you are a light to moderate drinker, the advice seems to be that it is reasonable to continue, provided you have your doctor's blessing, but the other risks associated with alcohol outweigh any advice to start drinking or to increase the amount of alcohol you drink. Remember, however, that alcohol is very fattening.

Regular exercise, such as golf, swimming, walking, jogging or cycling has substantial benefits.

MEAL PLANNING

If all your meals contain generous portions of fresh vegetables, fruit and starchy foods, together with small portions of dairy food or meat, fish and vegetarian alternatives, you cannot go too far wrong. Eating for a healthy heart does not mean certain foods are entirely forbidden, but it does mean:

• Cutting down on foods that contain a lot of fat, and saturated fat in particular, such as dairy products, meat products, cakes, biscuits, fatty snacks and confectionery, especially chocolate

• Switching to low-fat dairy produce, cooking with lean meat rather than eating meat pies or pasties, and eating plenty of fish, lean poultry, beans and pulses

• Using limited amounts of low-fat spreads and oils.

SAMPLE MENUS

Breakfast

Choose one of the following:

• Wholemeal toast with a thin scraping of low-fat spread and preserve
• Wholegrain cereal with skimmed milk (add fresh or dried fruit)
• Fruit (fresh or dried fruit compote) and low-fat natural yogurt
• Poached egg or fish, or boiled egg with wholemeal toast
• Wholemeal bun or muffin
• Porridge with skimmed milk.

Lunch

Try one of the following ideas:

• Wholemeal sandwiches or rolls with a small amount of lean meat, fish or cheese and lots of salad
• Vegetable-based soup with a wholemeal roll
• Rice or pasta salad
• A baked potato with a large mixed salad and a small amount of lean meat or cheese
• Baked beans on toast.

Main Meal

Try one of these suggestions:

• Hearty soup, such as minestrone or a vegetable broth
• Wholemeal pasta or risotto with vegetable-based sauce
• Grilled fish or meat plus vegetables and/or salad
• A baked potato with lean minced beef or pork chilli con carne (or vegetarian equivalent)
• A stir-fry made with a small amount of lean meat or fish with plenty of vegetables and using polyunsaturated oil, served with rice
• Vegetable and pulse or pasta casserole with wholemeal cobbler or potato topping
• A vegetable gratin made with a small amount of cheese.

Desserts

Use desserts to add more fruit and low-fat dairy produce to your diet. The following provide essential nutrients without excessive amounts of fat:

• Fresh fruit; fruit salad with yogurt or low-fat frozen yogurt (occasionally with ice cream)
• Canned fruit salad in fruit juice; dried fruit compote
• Bread and butter pudding or rice pudding (made with low-fat milk and added fruit)
• Wholemeal pancakes filled with fresh fruit purée
• Home-made fruit crumble
• Real fruit jelly, fresh fruit fool made with reduced-fat cream or yogurt or low-fat custard
• Fruit brûlée made with low-fat yogurt instead of cream
• Sorbet.

HEALTHY COOKING TECHNIQUES

The aims of cooking for a healthy heart are to avoid adding fat to food, to reduce the saturated fat content of the ingredients where possible, to use techniques that retain the vitamins and minerals and, of course, to ensure that the food is delicious by preserving or enhancing its flavour, colour and texture.

STIR-FRYING

This method means that food cooks quickly to retain maximum nutritional value, colour and texture.

Slivers of meat can be marinated in savoury mixtures of, for example, soy sauce, fruit juice such as lemon, tomato purée and vinegar, or similar sauces before cooking to tenderize them and add flavour.

Meat and/or vegetables need to be cut into small pieces, so that they cook quickly and evenly.

1 Always heat the wok or frying pan for a minute or so before adding the oil or any other ingredients.

STEAMING

Food is cooked over boiling liquid (usually water) but it does not touch the liquid. As a result most of the vitamins and minerals are retained. Browning is not part of the process, so fat need never be added.

Steaming preserves the texture of foods and is a good cooking method for those who prefer their vegetables with a bit of bite. It is also very useful for fish, poultry and puddings.

- Prepare ingredients as for stir-frying. Expandable steamers will fit a range of saucepan sizes. Put food straight into the steamer and cover.
- If using a bamboo steamer over either a wok or pan of boiling liquid, place the food in a bowl first, then cover.

2 Cut the meat and/or vegetables into thin slivers to minimize the cooking time. When adding the first ingredients, quickly reduce the heat a little. This will ensure that they are not overcooked or burnt by the time the remaining ingredients have been added.

MICROWAVING

This is a quick and useful way of cooking vegetables, fruit and fish. Naturally moist foods are cooked without additional liquid, and only a small amount of liquid is added to other foods. As a result, vitamins and minerals do not leach out into cooking water which is then thrown away. Fat is not required for cooking, and microwaved food can be seasoned with fresh chopped herbs instead of salt. The flavour can be sharpened by adding a little lemon juice.

- Place food in a microwave-proof dish, or wrap in a paper parcel. Refer to the manufacturer's handbook for information on power levels and cooking times.

3 Once all the ingredients have been added, quickly increase the heat to allow the dish to cook in the least possible time. This allows the ingredients to retain a crisp texture and prevents them from absorbing too much oil. Be careful not to burn the ingredients. Use a wooden spoon or non-stick slotted spoon to turn the ingredients as you stir-fry.

Microwaved jacket potatoes can be cooked in a fraction of the time necessary in a conventional oven.

CASSEROLING

One-pot meals are good for stress-free entertaining and are easy to prepare. They are not necessarily the heavy dishes you may imagine: some are light and fresh, using vegetables according to the season. They also have the advantage that vitamins and minerals are retained in the stock, which is served alongside the other ingredients, and are a delicious way of adding more fibre to your diet if you include pasta, grains and rice. Use only the minimum amount of fat for cooking and make the casserole a day ahead, then cool and chill it. Any fat will solidify on the surface and can easily be lifted off before the casserole is reheated.

PRESSURE COOKING

This method cuts cooking time dramatically, which encourages the frequent consumption of beneficial low-fat foods (brown rice cooks in 7 minutes, potatoes in 6). Like steaming, pressure cooking retains more nutrients because the food is not in contact with the cooking water.

GRILLING

There's no need to add fat when grilling meat, fish or vegetables. Use a rack and any fat that runs from the meat can easily be drained. Brush the rack with oil before cooking to prevent the food from sticking. Cook under a preheated grill and baste with lemon juice, if necessary.

POACHING

This is an excellent way of cooking delicate white fish (plaice) or whole oily fish (mackerel, salmon, trout). Fish steaks, particularly cod, halibut, salmon and tuna also cook well by either method and there is no need to add any fat.
- Poaching can be done either in the oven or on top of the cooker.

1 Trim visible fat from meat or remove skin from poultry.

2 Skim off all excess fat from the surface before reheating the dish.

- To oven-poach fish, pour in boiling liquid to barely cover the fish, add any flavourings and cover with buttered greaseproof paper. Cook in a preheated oven to 180°C/ 350°F/Gas 4.

- To poach on top of the cooker, suspend the fish in the poaching liquid, either in a muslin hammock or on a rack. Cover with liquid, bring to the boil and simmer gently until cooked.

Cook fish or meat on a rack so any excess fat drains away.

EQUIPMENT

There are various pieces of equipment which will help you to prepare food with a minimum amount of fat. Some do not need you to add any fat at all, others allow the fat to drain away.

STEAMERS

These may be oval or round and consist of two pans, a lower one, which holds the boiling water or stock and a perforated upper pan, which holds the food. Steam enters via the holes, and is trapped by a lid on the top pan. Metal steaming baskets that stand inside a saucepan are suitable for steaming small quantities of food. A metal colander sitting inside a saucepan can also be used as a steamer; find a saucepan lid which will fit on top, or make a lid from foil to cover. Bamboo steamers come in a range of sizes with multiple layers and will fit either over a saucepan or inside a wok. There are now electrical appliance steamers which are quick and efficient.

ROASTING GADGETS

Placing meat on a trivet or a rack in a roasting tin will allow any excess fat to drain away from the meat. Do not add fat. Cover the meat with aluminium foil if necessary to prevent it from drying out. Chicken roasters hold the chicken so that it stands upright in the roasting tin. This is a very efficient way of draining the fat while retaining all the taste and flavour of the chicken, keeping it moist at the same time.

PASTRY BRUSHES

These inexpensive items are useful for brushing pans and baking tins with a minimal amount of oil.

WOK

This is the perfect utensil for stir-frying. Thanks to its spherical shape, the heat spreads from the base upwards so all the ingredients receive an equal amount of heat. A new wok should be seasoned before it is first used. Wash and dry it thoroughly. Heat the dry wok, remove it from the heat and rub a little oil and salt on to the surface. Return it to a high heat, until the oil burns off. Allow to cool, wipe and use. It should not be necessary to wash the wok again, just wipe it clean after use.

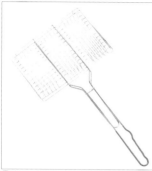

BARBECUE GRILL BASKETS

These allow food to be held securely when placed over the hot coals, at the same time allowing fat to drain away. Non-stick versions are available from most department stores.

NON-STICK PANS

Good quality non-stick frying pans, saucepans and grill pans allow food to be cooked by any method, even frying, without additional fat. Food can also be sweated or sautéed with the minimal amount of added fat. Pans with ribbed bases allow any fat that drains from meat to be poured away. Heavy-based cast-iron pans of good quality also allow cooking on the hob without added fat.

GRAVY SEPARATOR

Available as a glass or plastic jug or ceramic "boat", this item has a low-set spout that takes gravy from the bottom of the jug and avoids the fat floating on the surface of the gravy when pouring.

MOULI OR BLENDER

Use one of these handy appliances to purée vegetables in order to thicken sauces instead of adding a roux, cornflour or eggs. They are also excellent for thickening and lightly blending soups.

BULB BASTER

This works like a syringe when the bulb at the top is squeezed, sucking up fat from the roasting tin.

Although conventionally used as a means of basting a roast with fat, in the hands of a health-conscious cook the utensil proves ideal for skimming fat from soups, sauces and casseroles.

Above: Choose non-stick heavy-based pans, sturdy insulated handles and tight-fitting lids.

Opposite: Bamboo steamers.

Right: Various styles of woks and pans.

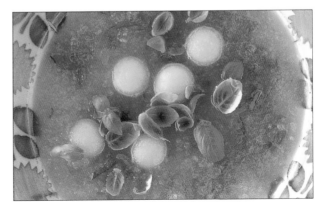

Soups and Starters

With abundant fresh vegetables available all the year round, it is easy to

include them as part of a healthy and imaginative diet. Soups will make a

substantial lunch served with crusty wholemeal or granary bread, or as a first

course. Try refreshing Melon and Basil Soup on a hot summer's day or warm

up in winter with spicy Leek, Parsnip and Ginger Soup. Colourful starters,

such as Aubergine, Roast Garlic and Red Pepper Pâté, and Broccoli and

Chestnut Terrine are an inspiring way to enjoy wholefoods

when entertaining.

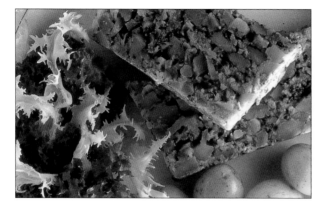

Melon and Basil Soup

A deliciously refreshing, chilled fruit soup, just right for a hot summer's day.

INGREDIENTS

Serves 4–6
2 Charentais or rock melons
75g/3oz/⅓ cup caster sugar
175ml/6fl oz/¾ cup water
finely grated rind and juice of 1 lime
45ml/3 tbsp shredded fresh basil
fresh basil leaves, to garnish

COOK'S TIP

Add the syrup in two stages, as the amount of sugar needed will depend on the sweetness of the melon.

1 Cut the melons in half across the middle. Scrape out the seeds and discard. Using a melon baller, scoop out 20–24 balls and set aside for the garnish. Scoop out the remaining flesh and then place in a blender or food processor.

2 Place the sugar, water and lime rind and half the juice in a pan over a low heat. Stir until dissolved, bring to the boil and simmer for 2–3 minutes. Remove from the heat and leave to cool. Pour half the mixture into the blender or food processor with the melon flesh. Blend until smooth, adding the remaining syrup and lime juice to taste. Pour the mixture into a bowl, stir in the basil and chill. Serve with basil leaves and melon balls.

NUTRITION NOTES

Per portion:

Energy	63Kcals/268kJ
Protein	0.28g
Fat	0.09g
Saturated Fat	0.0g
Carbohydrate	16g
Fibre	0.25g
Sugar	16.2g
Sodium	0.17g

Leek, Parsnip and Ginger Soup

A flavoursome winter warmer, with the added spiciness of fresh ginger. An ideal light supper dish.

INGREDIENTS

Serves 4–6
30ml/2 tbsp olive oil
225g/8oz leeks, sliced
25g/1oz fresh ginger root, finely chopped
675g/1½lb parsnips, roughly chopped
300ml/½ pint/1¼ cups dry white wine
1.2 litres/2 pints/5 cups vegetable stock or water
salt and freshly ground black pepper
low-fat fromage blanc, to garnish
paprika, to garnish

1 Heat the oil in a large pan and add the leeks and ginger. Cook gently for 2–3 minutes, just until the leeks start to soften.

NUTRITION NOTES

Per portion:	
Energy	165Kcals/692kJ
Protein	3.4g
Fat	6.5g
Saturated Fat	0.99g
Carbohydrate	16.4g
Fibre	6g
Sugar	8.2g
Sodium	0.17g

2 Add the chopped parsnips and cook for a further 7–8 minutes until just soft, stirring occasionally.

3 Pour in the wine and stock or water and bring to the boil. Reduce the heat and simmer for 20–30 minutes.

4 Purée in a blender until smooth. Season to taste. Reheat and garnish with a swirl of fromage blanc and a light dusting of paprika.

Broccoli and Almond Soup

The creaminess of the toasted almonds combines perfectly with the slight bitterness of the taste of fresh broccoli.

INGREDIENTS

Serves 4–6
50g/2oz/⅔ cup ground almonds
675g/1½lb broccoli
900ml/1½ pints/3¾ cups vegetable
    stock or water
300ml/½ pint/1¼ cups skimmed milk
salt and freshly ground black pepper

———— COOK'S TIP ————

Ground almonds can be bought already prepared from many foodstores.

1 Preheat the oven to 180°C/ 350°F/Gas 4. Spread the ground almonds evenly on a baking sheet and toast in the oven for about 10 minutes, or until golden. Reserve one-quarter of the almonds and set aside for the garnish.

2 Cut the broccoli into small florets and steam for 6–7 minutes or until just tender. Drain.

3 Place the remaining toasted almonds, broccoli, stock or water and milk in a blender and blend until smooth. Season to taste.

4 Reheat the soup, divide among warmed bowls and serve sprinkled with the reserved toasted almonds.

———— NUTRITION NOTES ————

Per portion:
Energy	104Kcals/436kJ
Protein	8.36g
Fat	5.7g
Saturated Fat	0.66g
Carbohydrate	5.1g
Fibre	3.5g
Sugar	4.5g
Sodium	0.03g

Red Onion and Beetroot Soup

This beautiful vivid ruby-red soup will look stunning at any dinner party.

INGREDIENTS

Serves 4–6
15ml/1 tbsp olive oil
350g/12oz red onions, sliced
2 garlic cloves, crushed
275g/10oz cooked beetroot, cut into sticks
1.2 litres/2 pints/5 cups vegetable stock or water
50g/2oz/1 cup cooked soup pasta
30ml/2 tbsp raspberry vinegar
salt and freshly ground black pepper
low-fat yogurt or fromage blanc, to garnish
snipped chives, to garnish

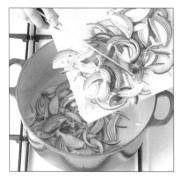

1 Heat the olive oil in a large casserole dish and add the onions and garlic.

NUTRITION NOTES	
Per portion:	
Energy	147Kcals/615kJ
Protein	5.2g
Fat	3.6g
Saturated Fat	0.5g
Carbohydrate	25g
Fibre	3.0g
Sugar	12.1g
Sodium	0.54g

2 Cook gently for about 20 minutes or until soft and tender.

COOK'S TIP

Try substituting cooked barley for the pasta to give extra nuttiness.

3 Add the beetroot, stock or water, cooked pasta shapes and vinegar and heat through. Season to taste.

4 Ladle into bowls. Top each one with a spoonful of yogurt or fromage blanc and sprinkle with the snipped chives.

Broccoli and Chestnut Terrine

Served hot or cold, this versatile terrine is suitable for a dinner party, a picnic or as a main course.

INGREDIENTS

Serves 4–6
450g/1lb broccoli, cut into small florets
225g/8oz cooked chestnuts, roughly chopped
50g/2oz/1 cup fresh wholemeal breadcrumbs
60ml/4 tbsp low-fat natural yogurt
30ml/2 tbsp Parmesan cheese, finely grated
salt, grated nutmeg and freshly ground black pepper
2 eggs, beaten

2 Blanch or steam the broccoli for 3–4 minutes until just tender. Drain well. Reserve one-quarter of the smallest florets and chop the rest finely.

5 Spoon the broccoli mixture into the prepared tin. Smooth so it retains an even surface and then place it in a roasting tin.

1 Preheat the oven to 180°C/350°F/Gas 4. Grease and line a 900g/2lb loaf tin with non-stick baking paper.

3 Mix together the chestnuts, breadcrumbs, yogurt and Parmesan, and season to taste.

6 Pour boiling water into the roasting tin to come halfway up the sides of the loaf tin. Bake for 20–25 minutes. Remove from the oven and tip out onto a plate or tray. Serve cut into even slices.

4 Fold in the chopped broccoli, reserved florets and the beaten eggs.

— NUTRITION NOTES —	
Per portion:	
Energy	164Kcals/691kJ
Protein	9.84g
Fat	5.8g
Saturated Fat	2.08g
Carbohydrate	19.29g
Fibre	3.97g
Sugar	4.65g
Sodium	0.14g

Pea Guacamole with Crudités

INGREDIENTS

Serves 4–6

350g/12oz/3 cups frozen peas,
   defrosted
1 garlic clove, crushed
2 spring onions, trimmed and chopped
5ml/1 tsp finely grated rind and juice
   of 1 lime
2.5ml/½ tsp ground cumin
dash of Tabasco sauce
15ml/1 tbsp reduced calorie
   mayonnaise
30ml/2 tbsp chopped fresh coriander
salt and freshly ground black pepper
pinch of paprika and lime slices, to
   garnish

For the crudités

6 baby carrots
2 celery sticks
1 red-skinned eating apple
1 pear
75g/30oz baby sweetcorn
15ml/1 tbsp lemon or lime juice
6 baby sweetcorn

1 Put the peas, garlic, spring onions, lime rind and juice, cumin, Tabasco sauce, mayonnaise and salt and freshly ground black pepper into a food processor or a blender for a few minutes and process until smooth.

2 Add the chopped fresh coriander and process for a few more seconds. Spoon into a serving bowl, cover with clear film and then chill in the refrigerator for 30 minutes, to let the flavours develop.

3 For the crudités, trim and peel the carrots. Halve the celery sticks lengthways and trim into sticks, the same length as the carrots. Quarter, core and thickly slice the apple and pear, then dip into the lemon or lime juice. Arrange with the baby sweetcorn on a platter.

4 Sprinkle the paprika over the guacamole and garnish with the lime slices.

NUTRITION NOTES	
Per portion:	
Energy	102Kcals/429kJ
Protein	483g
Fat	1.96g
Saturated Fat	0.22g
Carbohydrate	17.1g
Fibre	5.61g
Sugar	10g
Sodium	0.05g

Cheese-stuffed Pears

These pears, with their scrumptious creamy topping, make a sublime dish when served with a simple salad.

INGREDIENTS

Serves 4

50g/2oz/¼ cup ricotta cheese
50g/2oz/¼ cup dolcelatte cheese
15ml/1 tbsp honey
½ celery stick, finely sliced
8 green olives, pitted and roughly chopped
4 dates, stoned and cut into thin strips
pinch of paprika
4 ripe pears
150ml/¼ pint/⅔ cup apple juice

1 Preheat the oven to 200°C/ 400°F/Gas 6. Place the ricotta in a bowl and crumble in the dolcelatte. Add the rest of the ingredients except for the pears and apple juice and mix well.

NUTRITION NOTES	
Per portion:	
Energy	188.25Kcals/793kJ
Protein	4.67g
Fat	5.99g
Saturated Fat	3.28g
Carbohydrate	30.69g
Fibre	4.20g
Sugar	30.69g
Sodium	0.18g

2 Halve the pears lengthwise and use a melon baller to remove the cores. Place in an ovenproof dish and divide the filling equally among them.

3 Pour in the apple juice and cover the dish with foil. Bake for 20 minutes or until the pears are tender. Remove the foil and place the dish under a hot grill for 3 minutes. Serve immediately while hot.

Aubergine, Roast Garlic and Red Pepper Pâté

This is a simple pâté of smoky baked aubergine, sweet pink peppercorns and red peppers, with more than a hint of garlic!

INGREDIENTS

Serves 4
3 medium aubergines
2 red peppers
5 whole garlic cloves, unpeeled
7.5ml/1½ tsp pink peppercorns in brine, drained and crushed
30ml/2 tbsp chopped fresh coriander

1 Preheat the oven to 200°C/400°F/Gas 6. Arrange the whole aubergines, peppers and garlic cloves on a baking sheet and place in the oven. After 10 minutes remove the garlic cloves and turn over the aubergines and peppers.

2 Peel the garlic cloves and place in the bowl of a blender.

3 After a further 20 minutes remove the blistered and charred peppers from the oven and place in a plastic bag. Leave to cool.

4 After a further 10 minutes remove the aubergines from the oven. Split in half and scoop the flesh into a sieve placed over a bowl. Press the flesh with a spoon to remove the bitter juices.

5 Add the mixture to the garlic in the blender and blend until smooth. Place in a large mixing bowl.

6 Peel and chop the red peppers and stir into the aubergine mixture. Mix in the peppercorns and fresh coriander and serve at once.

— NUTRITION NOTES —	
Per portion:	
Energy	28Kcals/119kJ
Protein	1.63g
Fat	0.57g
Saturated Fat	0.13g
Carbohydrate	4.54g
Fibre	2.55g
Sugar	3.7g
Sodium	0.05g

FISH AND
SEAFOOD DISHES

The stunning array of fresh fish and seafood available in our fishmongers and supermarkets is a temptation all the year round. Fish is good for us, so experiment with different types, especially oily and white fish. Oily fish is particularly important for a healthy heart, with its protective "omega 3" fatty acids. Versatile white fish is low in calories and quick to prepare and cook. Try Lemon Sole en Papillote cooked in its own juices, Oatmeal-crusted Mackerel, or delicious Smoked Trout Cannelloni.

Lemon Sole en Papillote

Make sure that these paper parcels are well sealed, so that none of the delicious juices can escape.

INGREDIENTS

Serves 4
4 lemon sole fillets, each weighing
    about 150g/5oz
½ small cucumber, sliced
4 lemon slices
60ml/4 tbsp dry white wine, optional
sprigs of fresh dill, to garnish
new potatoes and braised celery,
    to serve

For the yogurt hollandaise
150ml/¼ pint/⅔ cup low-fat yogurt
5ml/1 tsp lemon juice
2 egg yolks
5ml/1 tsp Dijon mustard
salt and freshly ground black pepper

1 Preheat the oven to 180°C/350°F/Gas 4. Cut out four heart shapes from non-stick baking paper, each about 20 x 15cm/8 x 6in.

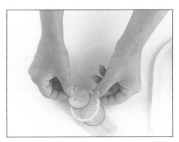

2 Place a sole fillet on one side of each heart. Arrange the cucumber and lemon slices on top of each fillet. Sprinkle with the wine, if using, and close the parcels by turning the edges of the paper and twisting to secure. Put on a baking tray and cook in the preheated oven for 15 minutes.

3 For the hollandaise, beat together the yogurt, lemon juice and egg yolks in a double boiler or bowl placed over a saucepan. Cook over simmering water, stirring for 15 minutes, or until thickened. (The sauce will become thinner after 10 minutes, but will thicken again.)

4 Remove from the heat and stir in the mustard. Season to taste. Open the fish parcels, garnish with a sprig of dill and serve accompanied with the sauce, new potatoes and braised celery.

NUTRITION NOTES	
Per portion:	
Energy	186Kcals/793kJ
Protein	29.5g
Fat	5.4g
Saturated Fat	1.25g
Carbohydrate	3.16g
Fibre	0.05g
Sugar	3.12g
Sodium	0.21g

Oatmeal-crusted Mackerel

An appetizing way of serving fresh mackerel. Serve with baked potatoes and cooked mange-touts for a tasty and filling meal.

INGREDIENTS

Serves 4
4 mackerel each weighing about
    175–225g/6–8oz
juice of 1 lemon
50g/2oz/½ cup fine oatmeal
50g/2oz/½ cup medium oatmeal
30ml/2 tbsp chopped fresh mixed herbs
salt and ground black pepper
tomato quarters and fresh herb sprigs,
    to garnish

1 Remove and discard the heads from the mackerel, gut and then clean the fish.

2 Sprinkle the inside of each mackerel with lemon juice and a little seasoning.

3 Mix together the oatmeals and herbs and press the oatmeal mixture firmly on to the outside of each fish.

4 Preheat the grill. Grill the fish under a fairly high heat for 6–8 minutes, turning once, until the fish is cooked and is just beginning to flake. Garnish with tomato quarters and fresh herb sprigs.

NUTRITION NOTES

Per portion:

Energy	480Kcals/2001kJ
Protein	36.30g
Fat	30.15g
Saturated Fat	6.18g
Carbohydrate	16.63g
Fibre	1.88g
Sugar	0.00g
Sodium	0.0g

COOK'S TIP

Sardines or trout can be used in place of the mackerel in this recipe and are equally healthy and tasty.

Smoked Trout Cannelloni

Smoked trout can be bought already filleted or whole. If you buy fillets, you'll need 225g/8oz of fish.

INGREDIENTS

Serves 4–6
1 large onion, finely chopped
1 garlic clove, crushed
60ml/4 tbsp vegetable stock
2 x 400g/14oz cans chopped tomatoes
2.5ml/½ tsp dried mixed herbs
1 smoked trout, weighing about
    400g/14oz
75g/3oz/¾ cup frozen peas, thawed
75g/3oz/1½ cups fresh breadcrumbs
16 cannelloni tubes
salt and freshly ground black pepper
mixed salad, to serve

For the cheese sauce
25g/1oz/2 tbsp low-fat spread
25g/1oz/¼ cup plain flour
350ml/12 fl oz/1½ cups skimmed milk
freshly grated nutmeg
15g/½oz/1½ tbsp freshly grated
    Parmesan cheese

2 Stir in the tomatoes and dried herbs. Simmer uncovered for a further 10 minutes, or until very thick.

3 Meanwhile, skin the smoked trout with a sharp knife. Carefully flake the flesh and discard all the bones. Mix the fish together with the tomato mixture, peas, breadcrumbs, salt and freshly ground black pepper.

5 For the sauce, put the low-fat spread, flour and milk into a saucepan and cook over a medium heat, whisking until the sauce thickens. Simmer for 2–3 minutes, stirring all the time. Season to taste with salt, freshly ground black pepper and nutmeg.

6 Pour the sauce over the cannelloni and sprinkle with the Parmesan cheese. Bake in the preheated oven for 35–40 minutes, or until the top is golden. Serve with a mixed salad.

1 Simmer the onion, garlic clove and stock in a large covered saucepan for 3 minutes. Uncover and continue to cook, stirring occasionally, until the stock has reduced entirely.

COOK'S TIP
You can use a 200g/7oz can of tuna in brine in place of the trout, if preferred.

4 Preheat the oven to 190°C/ 375°F/Gas 5. Spoon the filling into the cannelloni tubes and arrange in an ovenproof dish.

NUTRITION NOTES

Per portion:	
Energy	277Kcals/1172kJ
Protein	17.83g
Fat	5.15g
Saturated Fat	1.1g
Carbohydrate	42.3g
Fibre	3.07g
Sugar	9.21g
Sodium	0.25g

Herby Fishcakes with Lemon and Chive Sauce

The wonderful flavour of fresh herbs makes these fishcakes the catch of the day.

INGREDIENTS

Serves 4

350g/12oz potatoes, peeled
75ml/5 tbsp skimmed milk
350g/12oz haddock or hoki fillets, skinned and bones removed
15ml/1 tbsp lemon juice
15ml/1 tbsp creamed horseradish sauce
30ml/2 tbsp chopped fresh parsley
flour, for dusting
115g/4oz/2 cups fresh wholemeal breadcrumbs
salt and freshly ground black pepper
sprigs of flat leaf parsley, to garnish
mangetouts and a sliced tomato and onion salad, to serve

For the lemon and chive sauce

150ml/¼ pint/⅔ cup low-fat yogurt
5ml/1 tsp lemon juice
thinly pared rind and juice of ½ lemon
120ml/4 fl oz/½ cup dry white wine (optional)
2 thin slices fresh root ginger
10ml/2 tsp cornflour
30ml/2 tbsp snipped fresh chives

1 Cook the potatoes in a large saucepan of boiling water for 15–20 minutes. Drain and mash with the milk and season to taste.

2 Purée the fish together with the lemon juice and horseradish sauce in a blender or food processor. Mix together with the potatoes and parsley.

3 With floured hands, shape the mixture into eight fishcakes and coat with the breadcrumbs. Chill in the refrigerator for 30 minutes.

4 Cook the fishcakes under a preheated moderate grill for 5 minutes on each side, until browned.

5 To make the sauce, cut the lemon rind into julienne strips and put into a saucepan with the lemon juice, wine and ginger and season to taste.

6 Simmer uncovered for 6 minutes. Blend the cornflour with 15ml/ 1 tbsp of cold water. Add to the saucepan and simmer until clear. Stir in the chives before serving. Serve the sauce hot with the fishcakes, garnished with flat leaf parsley and accompanied with mangetouts and salad.

NUTRITION NOTES	
Per portion:	
Energy	266Kcals/1130kJ
Protein	27g
Fat	2.1g
Saturated Fat	0.4g
Carbohydrate	32g
Fibre	3.43g
Sugar	3.36g
Sodium	0.28g

Seafood Pasta Shells with Spinach Sauce

You'll need very large pasta shells, measuring about 4cm/1½in long for this dish; don't try stuffing smaller shells – they're much too fiddly!

Ingredients

Serves 4

15g/½oz/1 tbsp low-fat spread
8 spring onions, finely sliced
6 tomatoes
32 large dried pasta shells
225g/8oz/1 cup low-fat soft cheese
90ml/6 tbsp skimmed milk
pinch of freshly grated nutmeg
225g/8oz cooked, peeled prawns
175g/6oz can white crabmeat, drained
    and flaked
115g/4oz frozen chopped spinach,
    thawed and drained
salt and freshly ground black pepper

1 Preheat the oven to 150°C/ 300°F/Gas 2. Melt the low-fat spread in a small saucepan and gently cook the spring onions for 3–4 minutes, or until softened.

——— Nutrition Notes ———	
Per portion:	
Energy	363 Kcals/1539 KJ
Protein	34.94g
Fat	6.08g
Saturated Fat	2.09g
Carbohydrate	45g
Fibre	3.98g
Sugar	9.16g
Sodium	0.62g

2 Plunge the tomatoes into a saucepan of boiling water for 1 minute, then into a saucepan of cold water. Slip off the skins. Halve the tomatoes, remove the seeds and cores and roughly chop the flesh.

3 Cook the pasta shells in lightly salted boiling water for about 10 minutes, or until al dente. Drain well.

4 Put the low-fat soft cheese and skimmed milk into a saucepan and heat gently, stirring until blended. Season with salt, freshly ground black pepper and a pinch of nutmeg. Measure 30ml/2 tbsp of the sauce into a bowl.

5 Add the spring onions, tomatoes, prawns, and crabmeat to the bowl. Mix well. Spoon the filling into the shells and place in a single layer in a shallow ovenproof dish. Cover with aluminium foil and cook in the preheated oven for 10 minutes.

6 Stir the spinach into the remaining sauce. Bring to the boil and simmer gently for 1 minute, stirring all the time. Drizzle over the pasta shells and serve hot.

Asparagus with Crabmeat Sauce

The subtle flavour of fresh asparagus is enhanced by the equally delicate taste of crabmeat in this classic dish.

INGREDIENTS

Serves 4

450g/1lb asparagus, trimmed
15ml/1 tbsp vegetable oil
4 thin slices of fresh root ginger
2 garlic cloves, chopped
115g/4oz/⅔ cup fresh or thawed frozen
    white crabmeat
5ml/1 tsp dry sherry
150ml/¼ pint/⅔ cup semi-skimmed
    milk
15ml/1 tbsp cornflour
45ml/3 tbsp cold water
salt and ground white pepper
1 spring onion, thinly shredded,
    to garnish

1 Bring a large pan of lightly salted water to the boil. Poach the asparagus for about 5 minutes until just crisp-tender. Drain well and keep hot in a shallow serving dish.

2 Heat the oil in a non-stick frying pan or wok. Cook the ginger and garlic for 1 minute to release their flavour, then lift them out with a slotted spoon and discard them.

3 Add the crabmeat, sherry and milk to the flavoured oil and cook, stirring often, for 2 minutes.

4 In a small bowl, mix the cornflour to a paste with the water and add to the pan slowly. Cook, stirring constantly, until the sauce is thick and creamy. Season to-taste with salt and pepper, spoon over the asparagus, garnish with shreds of spring onion and serve.

---------- NUTRITION NOTES ----------

Per portion:

Energy	128 Kcals/533 KJ
Protein	10.6g
Fat	5.6g
Saturated Fat	0.9g
Carbohydrate	8.9g
Fibre	2.0g
Sugar	4.2g
Sodium	0.25g

Smoked Haddock in Parsley Sauce

The toasted almond flakes complement the delicious flavour of the haddock in this recipe.

INGREDIENTS

Serves 4

450g/1lb smoked haddock fillet
1 small leek or onion, sliced thickly
300ml/½ pint/1¼ cups skimmed milk
a bouquet garni (bay leaf, thyme and
     parsley stalks)
25g/1oz/2 tbsp low-fat margarine
25g/1oz plain flour
225g/8oz pasta shells
30ml/2 tbsp chopped fresh parsley
salt and ground black pepper
15g/½oz toasted flaked almonds,
     to serve, optional

1 Remove all the skin and any bones from the haddock. Put into a pan with the leek or onion, milk and bouquet garni. Bring to the boil, cover and simmer gently for about 8–10 minutes until the fish flakes easily.

NUTRITION NOTES

Per portion:

Energy	361Kcals/1526kJ
Protein	31.2g
Fat	4.5g
Saturated Fat	0.9g
Carbohydrate	51.9g
Fibre	2.6g
Sugar	5.6g
Sodium	0.15g

2 Strain, reserving the milk for making the sauce, and discard the bouquet garni.

3 Put the margarine, flour and reserved milk into a pan. Bring to the boil and whisk until smooth. Season and add the fish and leek or onion.

4 Cook the pasta in a large pan of boiling water until al dente. Drain thoroughly and stir into the sauce with the chopped parsley. Serve immediately, scattered with almonds, if you like.

Hot Spicy Prawns with Campanelle

Tiger prawns are more expensive than normal prawns but make this an extra special meal.

INGREDIENTS

Serves 4–6

225g/8oz tiger prawns, cooked and peeled
1–2 garlic cloves, crushed
finely grated rind of 1 lemon
15ml/1 tbsp lemon juice
1.5ml/¼ tsp red chilli paste or large pinch dried ground chilli
15ml/1 tbsp light soy sauce
150g/5oz smoked turkey rashers
1 shallot or small onion, finely chopped
60ml/4 tbsp white wine
225g/8oz campanelle
60ml/4 tbsp fish stock
4 firm ripe tomatoes, skinned, seeded and chopped
30ml/2 tbsp chopped fresh parsley
salt and freshly ground black pepper

1 In a glass bowl, mix the prawns with the garlic, lemon rind and juice, chilli paste or ground chilli and soy sauce. Season with salt and pepper, cover and marinate the prawns for at least 1 hour.

2 Grill the turkey rashers, then cut them into 5mm/¼in dice.

3 Put the shallot or onion and white wine into a pan, bring to the boil, cover and cook for 2–3 minutes or until tender and the wine has reduced by half.

4 Cook the campanelle in a large pan of boiling, salted water until al dente. Drain thoroughly.

5 Just before serving, put the prawns with their marinade into a large frying pan, bring to the boil quickly and add the smoked turkey and fish stock. Heat through for 1 minute.

6 Add to the pasta with the chopped tomatoes and parsley, toss quickly and serve immediately.

NUTRITION NOTES	
Per portion:	
Energy	207Kcals/882kJ
Protein	17.5g
Fat	1.64g
Saturated Fat	0.25g
Carbohydrate	31.2g
Fibre	2.2g
Sugar	3.72g
Sodium	0.31g

MEAT AND POULTRY DISHES

You can enjoy lean cuts of meat as part of a healthy diet. Make the most of them in appetizing, low-fat recipes with plenty of seasonal vegetables and rice, pasta or potatoes to balance the meal. Use super-lean pork tenderloin to prepare Honey-Roast Pork with Thyme and Rosemary, or take advantage of the versatility of low-fat turkey and chicken to choose from our healthy versions of Turkey Tonnato, Turkey and Tomato Hot-pot and Chicken with Orange and Mustard Sauce.

Turkey Tonnato

This low-fat version of the Italian dish 'vitello tonnato' is garnished with strips of red pepper instead of the traditional anchovy fillets.

Ingredients

Serves 4
450g/1lb turkey fillets
1 small onion, sliced
1 bay leaf
4 black peppercorns
350ml/12fl oz/1½ cups chicken stock
200g/7oz can tuna in brine, drained
75ml/5 tbsp reduced-calorie
  mayonnaise
30ml/2 tbsp lemon juice
2 red peppers, seeded and thinly sliced
about 25 capers, drained
pinch of salt
salad, lemon wedges and tomatoes,
  to serve

1 Put the turkey fillets in a single layer in large, heavy-based saucepan. Add the onion, bay leaf, peppercorns and stock. Bring to the boil and reduce the heat. Cover and simmer for 12 minutes, or until tender.

2 Turn off the heat and leave the turkey to cool in the stock, then remove with a slotted spoon. Slice thickly and arrange on a serving plate.

3 Boil the stock until reduced to about 75ml/5 tbsp. Strain and leave to cool.

Put the tuna, mayonnaise, lemon juice, 45ml/3 tbsp of the reduced stock and salt into a blender or food processor and purée until smooth.

5 Stir in enough of the remaining stock to reduce the sauce to the thickness of double cream. Spoon over the turkey.

6 Arrange the strips of red pepper in a lattice pattern over the turkey. Put a caper in the centre of each square. Chill in the refrigerator for 1 hour and serve with a fresh mixed salad and tomatoes and lemon wedges.

Nutrition Notes

Per portion:

Energy	239Kcals/1004kJ
Protein	38.45g
Fat	7.55g
Saturated Fat	0.69g
Carbohydrate	4.45g
Fibre	0.58g
Sugar	3.2g
Sodium	0.41g

Turkey and Tomato Hot-pot

Turkey is not just for festive occasions. Here, it's turned into tasty meatballs and simmered with rice in a tomato sauce.

INGREDIENTS

Serves 4

25g/1oz white bread, crusts removed
30ml/2 tbsp skimmed milk
1 garlic clove, crushed
2.5ml/½ tsp caraway seeds
225g/8oz minced turkey
1 egg white
350ml/12fl oz/1½ cups chicken stock
400g/14oz can plum tomatoes
15ml/1 tbsp tomato purée
90g/3½oz/½ cup easy-cook rice
salt and freshly ground black pepper
15ml/1 tbsp chopped fresh basil,
 to garnish
carrot and courgette ribbons, to serve

1 Cut the bread into small cubes and put into a mixing bowl. Sprinkle over the milk and leave to soak for about 5 minutes.

COOK'S TIP

To make carrot and courgette ribbons, cut the vegetables lengthways into thin strips using a vegetable peeler, then blanch or steam until cooked through.

2 Add the garlic, caraway seeds, turkey, salt and freshly ground black pepper to the bread. Mix together well.

3 Whisk the egg white until stiff, then fold, half at a time, into the turkey mixture. Chill for 10 minutes in the refrigerator.

4 Put the stock, tomatoes and tomato purée into a large, heavy-based saucepan and bring to the boil.

5 Add the rice, stir and cook briskly for about 5 minutes. Turn the heat down to a gentle simmer.

6 Meanwhile, shape the turkey mixture into 16 small balls. Carefully drop them into the tomato stock and simmer for a further 8–10 minutes, or until the turkey balls and rice are cooked. Garnish with chopped basil, and serve with carrot and courgette ribbons.

NUTRITION NOTES

Per portion:
Energy	187Kcals/789kJ
Protein	17.54g
Fat	1.73g
Saturated Fat	0.42g
Carbohydrate	25.45g
Fibre	1.34g
Sugar	4.18g
Sodium	0.28g

Chicken with Orange and Mustard Sauce

The beauty of this recipe is its simplicity; the chicken continues to cook in its own juices while you prepare the sauce.

INGREDIENTS

Serves 4
4 chicken breasts, boned and skinned
5ml/1 tsp sunflower oil
salt and freshly ground black pepper
new potatoes and sliced courgettes
    tossed in parsley, to serve

For the orange and mustard sauce
2 large oranges
10ml/2 tsp cornflour
150ml/¼ pint/⅔ cup strained yogurt
5ml/1 tsp Dijon mustard

1 Peel the oranges using a sharp knife, removing all the white pith. Remove the segments by cutting between the membranes, holding the fruit over a small bowl to catch any juice. Set aside the segments with the juice until required.

2 Season the chicken with salt and freshly ground black pepper. Heat the oil in a non-stick frying pan and cook the chicken for 5 minutes on each side. Take out of the frying pan and wrap in foil; the meat will continue to cook for a while.

3 For the sauce, blend together the cornflour with the juice from the orange. Add the yogurt and mustard. Put into the frying pan and slowly bring to the boil. Simmer for 1 minute.

4 Add the orange segments to the sauce and heat gently. Unwrap the chicken and add any excess juices to the sauce. Slice on the diagonal and serve with the sauce, new potatoes and sliced courgettes tossed in parsley.

NUTRITION NOTES	
Per portion:	
Energy	236Kcals/1120kJ
Protein	44.5g
Fat	4.61g
Saturated Fat	1.13g
Carbohydrate	12.03g
Fibre	1.36g
Sugar	9.71g
Sodium	0.14g

Lamb with Vegetables

INGREDIENTS

Serves 6
Juice of 1 lemon
15ml/1 tbsp soy sauce
15ml/1 tbsp dry sherry, optional
1 garlic clove, crushed
10ml/2 tsp chopped fresh rosemary
6 lean chump or loin lamb chops
1 red onion, cut into 8 pieces
1 onion, cut into 8 pieces
1 red, 1 yellow and 1 green pepper,
    seeded and cut into chunks
4 courgettes, thickly sliced
350g/12oz button mushrooms
30ml/2 tbsp olive oil
4 plum tomatoes, peeled
400g/14oz can baby sweetcorn
60ml/4 tbsp chopped fresh basil
15-30ml/1-2 tbsp balsamic vinegar
salt and ground black pepper
fresh herbs and basil, to garnish

1 In a shallow dish, mix together the lemon juice, soy sauce, sherry, if using, garlic and rosemary. Coat the lamb chops in the marinade. Cover and refrigerate for 2 hours.

2 Preheat the oven to 200°C/ 400°F/Gas 6. Put the onions, peppers, courgettes and mushrooms in a roasting tin, drizzle over the olive oil and toss the vegetables to coat. Bake for 25 minutes.

3 Quarter the tomatoes and stir in with the sweetcorn. Bake for a further 10 minutes, until the vegetables are just tender and tinged at the edges. Add the basil, sprinkle over the balsamic vinegar and season to taste, stirring to mix.

4 Preheat the grill. Place the lamb chops under a medium grill for about 6 minutes on each side until cooked, turning over once. Brush the chops with any remaining marinade whilst they are cooking, to prevent them from drying out. Serve the chops with the cooked vegetables and garnish with fresh chopped herbs and a basil sprig.

NUTRITION NOTES	
Per portion:	
Energy	273Kcals/1143kJ
Protein	26.95g
Fat	12.60g
Saturated Fat	4.22g
Carbohydrate	13.15g
Fibre	4.99g
Sugar	0.10g
Sodium	0.91g

Honey-roast Pork with Thyme and Rosemary

Herbs and honey add flavour and
sweetness to tenderloin – the
leanest cut of pork.

INGREDIENTS

Serves 4

450g/1lb pork tenderloin
30ml/2 tbsp thick honey
30ml/2 tbsp Dijon mustard
5ml/1 tsp chopped fresh rosemary
2.5ml/½ tsp chopped fresh thyme
1.5ml/¼ tsp whole peppercorns
sprigs of fresh rosemary and thyme, to
  garnish
potato gratin and cauliflower, to serve

For the red onion confit

4 red onions
350ml/12fl oz/1½ cups vegetable stock
15ml/1 tbsp red wine vinegar
15ml/1 tbsp caster sugar
1 garlic clove, crushed
30ml/2 tbsp ruby port
pinch of salt

1 Preheat the oven to 180°C/
350°F/Gas 4. Trim off any visible
fat from the pork. Put the honey,
mustard, fresh rosemary and thyme in a
small bowl and mix them together well.

2 Crush the peppercorns using a
pestle and mortar. Spread the
honey mixture over the pork and
sprinkle with the crushed peppercorns.
Place in a non-stick roasting tin and
cook in the preheated oven for
approximately 35–45 minutes.

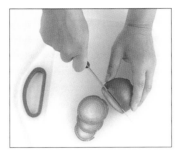

3 For the red onion confit, slice the
onions into rings and put them
into a heavy-based saucepan.

4 Add the stock, vinegar, sugar and
garlic clove to the saucepan. Bring
to the boil, then reduce the heat. Cover
and simmer for 15 minutes.

5 Uncover and pour in the port and
continue to simmer, stirring
occasionally, until the onions are soft
and the juices thick and syrupy. Season
to taste with salt.

6 Cut the pork into slices and
arrange on four warmed plates.
Serve hot, garnished with rosemary
and thyme and accompanied by the
red onion confit, potato gratin and
cauliflower.

NUTRITION NOTES

Per portion:

Energy	248.75Kcals/1043.25kJ
Protein	26.15g
Fat	8.12g
Saturated Fat	2.63g
Carbohydrate	16.42g
Fibre	0.87g
Sugar	14.54g
Sodium	0.28g

Hot and Sour Pork

Chinese five-spice powder is
made from a mixture of ground
star anise, Szechuan pepper,
cassia, cloves and fennel seed and
has a flavour similar to liquorice.
If you can't find any, use mixed
spice instead.

INGREDIENTS

Serves 4
350g/12oz pork fillet
5ml/1 tsp sunflower oil
2.5cm/1 in piece root ginger, grated
1 red chilli, seeded and finely chopped
5ml/1 tsp Chinese five-spice powder
15ml/1 tbsp sherry vinegar
15ml/1 tbsp soy sauce
225g/8oz can pineapple chunks in
    natural juice
175ml/6fl oz/¾ cup chicken stock
20ml/4 tsp cornflour
1 small green pepper, seeded and sliced
115g/4oz baby sweetcorn, halved
salt and freshly ground black pepper
sprig of flat leaf parsley, to garnish
boiled rice, to serve

1 Preheat the oven to 160°C/
325°F/Gas 3. Trim away any visible
fat from the pork and cut into 1cm/
½ in thick slices.

2 Brush the sunflower oil over the
base of a flameproof casserole. Heat
at a medium temperature, then fry the
meat for about 2 minutes on each side
or until lightly browned.

3 Blend together the ginger, chilli,
Chinese five-spice powder, vinegar
and soy sauce.

4 Drain the pineapple chunks,
reserving the juice. Make the stock
up to 300ml/½ pint/1¼ cups with the
reserved juice, mix together with the
spices and pour over the pork.

5 Slowly bring to the boil. Blend the
cornflour with 15ml/1 tbsp of cold
water and gradually stir into the pork.
Add the vegetables and season to taste.

6 Cover and cook in the oven for 30
minutes. Stir in the pineapple and
cook for a further 5 minutes. Garnish
with flat leaf parsley and serve with
boiled rice.

NUTRITION NOTES

Per portion:

Energy	194.25Kcals/815.25kJ
Protein	21.04g
Fat	7.39g
Saturated Fat	2.22g
Carbohydrate	11.36g
Fibre	0.82g
Sugar	7.87g
Sodium	0.36g

VEGETARIAN MAIN COURSE DISHES

An ideal way to increase the fresh vegetables and pulses necessary for a healthy diet is to include some vegetarian meals. Vegetarian dishes are full of flavour and use a variety of ingredients easily available and often quick to prepare. Boost your fibre intake with Vegetarian Cassoulet or enjoy the contrasting textures of Chilli Bean Bake with its cornbread topping. Mixed Vegetables Monk-style combines delicious Chinese vegetables and, if you're entertaining, Carrot Mousse with Mushroom Sauce would be a perfect choice.

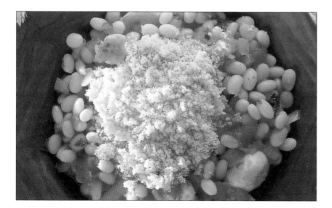

Carrot Mousse with Mushroom Sauce

Ingredients

Serves 4

350g/12oz carrots, roughly chopped
1 small red pepper, seeded and roughly
    chopped
45ml/3 tbsp vegetable stock or water
2 eggs
1 egg white
115g/4oz/½ cup quark or low-fat soft
    cheese
15ml/1 tbsp chopped fresh tarragon
salt and freshly ground black pepper
sprigs of fresh tarragon, to garnish
boiled rice and leeks, to serve

For the mushroom sauce

25g/1oz/2 tbsp low-fat spread
175g/6oz mushrooms, sliced
30ml/2 tbsp plain flour
250ml/8fl oz/1 cup skimmed milk

1 Preheat the oven to 190°C/
375°F/Gas 5. Line the bases of four
150ml/¼ pint/⅔ cup dariole moulds or
ramekin dishes with non-stick baking
paper. Put the carrots and red pepper in
a small saucepan with the vegetable
stock or water. Cover and cook for
5 minutes, or until tender. Drain well.

2 Lightly beat the eggs and egg white
together. Mix with the quark or
low-fat soft cheese. Season to taste.
Purée the cooked vegetables in a food
processor or blender. Add the cheese
mixture and process for a few seconds
more, until smooth. Stir in the
chopped tarragon.

3 Divide the carrot mixture between
the prepared dariole moulds or
ramekin dishes and cover with foil.
Place the dishes in a roasting tin half-
filled with hot water. Bake in the
preheated oven for 35 minutes, or
until set.

4 For the mushroom sauce, melt
15g/½ oz/1 tbsp of the low-fat
spread in a frying pan. Add the
mushrooms and gently sauté them
for 5 minutes, until soft.

5 Put the remaining low-fat spread in
a small saucepan together with the
flour and milk. Cook over a medium
heat, stirring all the time, until the
sauce thickens. Stir in the mushrooms
and season to taste.

6 Turn out each mousse on to a
serving plate. Spoon over a little
mushroom sauce and serve the
remainder separately. Garnish with a
sprig of fresh tarragon and serve with
boiled rice and leeks.

NUTRITION NOTES	
Per portion:	
Energy	179.75Kcals/753.25kJ
Protein	13.43g
Fat	6.53g
Saturated Fat	1.85g
Carbohydrate	17.77g
Fibre	2.81g
Sugar	11.29g
Sodium	0.17g

Cheese and Onion Slice

This inexpensive supper dish is made substantial with the addition of porridge oats.

INGREDIENTS

Serves 6
2 large onions, thinly sliced
1 garlic clove, crushed
150ml/¼ pint/⅔ cup vegetable stock
5ml/1 tsp vegetable extract
250g/9oz/3 cups porridge oats
115g/4oz/1 cup grated Edam cheese
30ml/2 tbsp chopped fresh parsley
2 eggs, lightly beaten
1 medium potato, peeled
salt and freshly ground black pepper
coleslaw and halved tomatoes, to serve

1 Preheat the oven to 180°C/350°F/Gas 4. Line the base of a 20cm/8in sandwich tin with non-stick baking paper. Put the onions, garlic clove and stock into a heavy-based saucepan and simmer until the stock has reduced entirely. Stir in the vegetable extract.

2 Spread the oats on a baking sheet and toast in the oven for 10 minutes. Mix with the onions, cheese, parsley, eggs, salt and freshly ground black pepper.

3 Thinly slice the potato and use it to line the base of the tin. Spoon in the oat mixture. Cover with a piece of tin foil.

4 Bake in the preheated oven for 35 minutes. Turn out on to a baking sheet and remove the lining paper. Put under a preheated hot grill to brown the potatoes. Cut into wedges and serve hot with the coleslaw and halved tomatoes, garnished with parsley.

NUTRITION NOTES	
Per portion:	
Energy	287.7Kcals/1210.5kJ
Protein	13.61g
Fat	10.83g
Saturated Fat	3.67g
Carbohydrate	36.17g
Fibre	3.66g
Sugar	1.21g
Sodium	0.24g

Leek and Caraway Gratin

Tender leeks are mixed with a creamy caraway sauce and a crunchy carrot topping.

INGREDIENTS

Serves 4–6
675g/1½lb leeks, cut into chunks
150ml/¼ pint/⅔ cup vegetable stock
45ml/3 tbsp dry white wine
5ml/1 tsp caraway seeds
pinch of salt
300ml/½ pint/1¼ cups skimmed milk
  as required
25g/1oz/2 tbsp polyunsaturated
  margarine
25g/1oz/¼ cup plain flour
115g/4oz/2 cups fresh wholemeal
  breadcrumbs
115g/4oz/1 cup grated carrot
30ml/2 tbsp chopped fresh parsley
75g/3oz Jarlsberg cheese, grated
25g/1oz/2 tbsp slivered almonds

1 Place the leeks in a large pan. Add the vegetable stock, wine, caraway seeds and salt. Bring to a simmer, cover and cook for 5–7 minutes until the leeks are just tender.

2 With a slotted spoon, transfer the leeks to an ovenproof dish. Reduce the remaining liquid to half then make the amount up to 350ml/12fl oz/1½ cups with skimmed milk.

3 Preheat the oven to 180°C/ 350°F/Gas 4. Melt the margarine in a saucepan, stir in the flour and cook without allowing it to colour for 1–2 minutes. Gradually add the stock and milk, stirring well, until you have a smooth sauce. Simmer for 5–6 minutes then pour over the leeks in the dish.

4 Mix together the breadcrumbs, carrot, parsley, Jarlsberg cheese and slivered almonds in a bowl and sprinkle over the leeks. Bake for 20–25 minutes until golden.

— NUTRITION NOTES —	
Per portion:	
Energy	193.83Kcals/813kJ
Protein	10.85g
Fat	8.52g
Saturated Fat	2.04g
Carbohydrate	18.75g
Fibre	4.73g
Sugar	6.93g
Sodium	0.16g

Vegetarian Cassoulet

Every town in south-west France has its own version of this popular classic dish. Warm, crusty French bread is all that is needed to complete this hearty vegetarian version.

INGREDIENTS

Serves 4–6
400g/14oz/2 cups dried haricot beans
1 bay leaf
2 onions
3 whole cloves
2 garlic cloves, crushed
5ml/1 tsp olive oil
2 leeks, thickly sliced
12 baby carrots
115g/4oz button mushrooms
400g/14oz can chopped tomatoes
15ml/1 tbsp tomato purée
5ml/1 tsp paprika
15ml/1 tbsp chopped fresh thyme
30ml/2 tbsp chopped fresh parsley
115g/4oz/2 cups fresh white
   breadcrumbs
salt and freshly ground black pepper

1 Soak the beans overnight in plenty of cold water. Drain and rinse under cold running water. Put them in a saucepan together with 1.75 litres/3 pints/7½ cups of cold water and the bay leaf. Bring to the boil and cook rapidly for 10 minutes.

2 Peel one of the onions and spike with cloves. Add to the beans and reduce the heat. Cover and simmer gently for 1 hour, until the beans are almost tender. Drain, reserving the stock but discarding the bay leaf and onion.

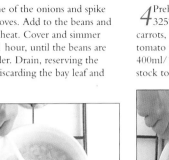

3 Chop the remaining onion and put it into a large flameproof casserole together with the garlic cloves and olive oil. Cook gently for 5 minutes, or until just softened.

NUTRITION NOTES	
Per portion:	
Energy	305.5Kcals/1296kJ
Protein	18.8g
Fat	3.33g
Saturated Fat	0.58g
Carbohydrate	53.3g
Fibre	16.33g
Sugar	12.16g
Sodium	0.2g

4 Preheat the oven to 160°C/325°F/Gas 3. Add the leeks, carrots, mushrooms, chopped tomatoes, tomato purée, paprika, thyme and 400ml/14fl oz/1⅔ cups of the reserved stock to the casserole.

5 Bring to the boil, cover and simmer gently for 10 minutes. Stir in the cooked beans and parsley. Season to taste.

6 Sprinkle with the breadcrumbs and bake uncovered in the preheated oven for 35 minutes, or until the topping is golden brown and crisp.

Almost-dry Roasted Vegetables

This is a delicious if rather slow method of cooking vegetables, but they retain all their juicy flavour. Serve them with pasta, hot toast or grilled polenta as a filling main course.

INGREDIENTS

Serves 4
1 aubergine
2 courgettes
1 yellow pepper
1 red pepper
4 garlic cloves
1 sweet red onion
1 small fennel bulb
20 asparagus spears
10 fresh basil leaves, roughly torn
45ml/3 tbsp extra virgin olive oil
15ml/1 tbsp balsamic vinegar
salt and freshly ground black pepper
sprigs of basil, to garnish

1 Preheat the oven to 240°C/ 475°F/Gas 9. Cut the aubergine and courgettes into 1cm/½in slices. Halve the peppers, discard the seeds and core, then cut them into chunks.

2 Finely chop the garlic and cut the onion into eight wedges.

3 Remove the root from the fennel and slice into 2.5cm/1in strips. Peel off any woody parts of the stems of the asparagus.

4 Place all the vegetables in a bowl, add the basil, then stir in the olive oil. Season with salt and pepper and mix together well.

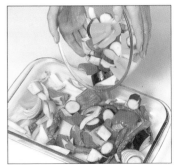

5 Tip the vegetables into a shallow roasting dish and roast in the oven for 30–40 minutes until all the vegetables are brown on the edges. Leave to cool, then sprinkle with the balsamic vinegar and serve garnished with the sprigs of basil.

NUTRITION NOTES	
Per portion:	
Energy	153Kcals/634kJ
Protein	5.4g
Fat	9.6g
Saturated Fat	1.2g
Carbohydrate	0.0g
Fibre	5.7g
Sugar	10.2g
Sodium	0.11g

COOK'S TIP
Aubergines can soak up oil quite quickly so check on the vegetables during the cooking time.

Ratatouille Penne Bake

This is a delicious savoury recipe ideal for a quick supper.

INGREDIENTS

Serves 6
1 small aubergine, cubed
2 courgettes, sliced
200g/7oz firm tofu, cubed
30ml/2 tbsp dark soy sauce
3 garlic cloves, crushed
10ml/2 tsp sesame seeds
30ml/2 tbsp olive oil
1 small red pepper, seeded and sliced
1 onion, finely chopped
150ml/¼ pint/⅔ cup vegetable stock
3 firm ripe tomatoes, skinned, seeded
  and quartered
15ml/1 tbsp chopped mixed herbs
225g/8oz penne
salt and ground black pepper
crusty bread, to serve

1 Place the aubergine and courgettes in a colander. Sprinkle with salt and leave to drain for 30 minutes, then rinse well and pat dry.

2 Mix the tofu with the soy sauce, one of the garlic cloves and sesame seeds. Cover and marinate for 30 minutes. Meanwhile, sauté the aubergine and courgettes in the olive oil until lightly browned.

3 Put the pepper, onion and remaining garlic into a saucepan with the stock. Bring to the boil, cover and cook for 5 minutes until tender. Remove the lid and boil until all the stock has evaporated. Add the tomatoes and herbs and cook for a further 3 minutes. Season to taste.

4 Meanwhile cook the pasta in a large pan of boiling, salted water until *al dente*. Drain thoroughly. Toss the pasta with all the vegetables and tofu. Transfer to a shallow 25cm/10in square ovenproof dish and grill until lightly toasted. Transfer to a serving dish and serve with warm crusty bread.

NUTRITION NOTES	
Per portion:	
Energy	234Kcals/986kJ
Protein	9.03g
Fat	8.4g
Saturated Fat	1.19g
Carbohydrate	32.6g
Fibre	2.6g
Sugar	5.3g
Sodium	0.34g

Chilli Bean Bake

The contrasting textures of beans, vegetables and crunchy cornbread topping make this a memorable meal.

INGREDIENTS

Serves 4

225g/8oz/1¼ cups red kidney beans
1 bay leaf
1 large onion, finely chopped
1 garlic clove, crushed
2 celery sticks, sliced
5ml/1 tsp ground cumin
5ml/1 tsp chilli powder
400g/14oz can chopped tomatoes
15ml/1 tbsp tomato purée
5ml/1 tsp dried mixed herbs
15ml/1 tbsp lemon juice
1 yellow pepper, seeded and diced
salt and freshly ground black pepper
mixed salad, to serve

For the cornbread topping
175g/6oz/1½ cups cornmeal
15ml/1 tbsp wholemeal flour
5ml/1 tsp baking powder
1 egg, beaten
175ml/6fl oz/¾ cup skimmed milk

1 Soak the beans overnight in cold water. Drain and rinse well. Pour 1 litre/1¾ pints/4 cups of water into a large, heavy-based saucepan together with the beans and bay leaf and boil rapidly for 10 minutes. Lower the heat, cover and simmer for 35–40 minutes, or until the beans are tender.

2 Add the onion, garlic clove, celery, cumin, chilli powder, chopped tomatoes, tomato purée and mixed herbs. Half-cover the pan with a lid and simmer for a further 10 minutes.

3 Stir in the lemon juice, yellow pepper and seasoning. Simmer for a further 8–10 minutes, stirring occasionally, until all the vegetables are just tender. Discard the bay leaf and then spoon the mixture into a large casserole dish.

4 Preheat the oven to 220°C/ 425°F/Gas 7. For the topping, put the cornmeal, flour, baking powder and a pinch of salt into a bowl and mix together. Make a well in the centre and add the egg and milk. Mix, and pour over the bean mixture. Bake in the preheated oven for 20 minutes, or until brown. Serve with a mixed salad.

─── NUTRITION NOTES ───	
Per portion:	
Energy	396.75Kcals/1676kJ
Protein	22.73g
Fat	4.67g
Saturated Fat	0.65g
Carbohydrate	68.75g
Fibre	11.9g
Sugar	9.89g
Sodium	0.27g

Mixed Vegetables Monk-style

Chinese monks eat neither meat nor fish, so "Monk-style" dishes are fine for vegetarians.

Ingredients

Serves 4

50g/2oz dried bean curd sticks
115g/4oz fresh lotus root, or 50g/2oz dried
10g/¼oz dried wood ears
8 dried Chinese mushrooms
15ml/1 tbsp vegetable oil
75g/3oz/¾ cup drained, canned straw mushrooms
115g/4oz/1 cup baby corn cobs, cut in half
30ml/2 tbsp light soy sauce
15ml/1 tbsp dry sherry
10ml/2 tsp caster sugar
150ml/¼ pint/⅔ cup vegetable stock
75g/3oz/¾ cup mangetouts, trimmed and cut in half
5ml/1 tsp cornflour
15ml/1 tbsp cold water
salt, to taste

1 Put the bean curd sticks in a bowl. Cover with hot water and leave to soak for 1 hour. If using fresh lotus root, peel it and slice it; if using dried lotus root, place it in a bowl of hot water and leave to soak for 1 hour.

Cook's Tip

The flavour of this tasty vegetable mix improves on keeping, so any leftovers would taste even better on the next day.

2 Prepare the wood ears and dried Chinese mushrooms by soaking them in separate bowls of hot water for 15 minutes. Drain the wood ears, trim off and discard the hard base from each and cut the rest into bite-size pieces. Drain the soaked mushrooms, trim off and discard the stems and chop the caps roughly.

3 Drain the bean curd sticks. Cut them into 5cm/2in long pieces, discarding any hard pieces. If using dried lotus root, drain well.

4 Heat the oil in a non-stick frying pan or wok. Stir-fry the wood ears, Chinese mushrooms and lotus root for about 30 seconds.

5 Add the pieces of bean curd sticks, straw mushrooms, baby corn cobs, soy sauce, sherry, caster sugar and stock. Bring to the boil, then cover the pan or wok, lower the heat and simmer for about 20 minutes.

6 Stir in the mangetouts, with salt to taste and cook, uncovered, for 2 minutes more. Mix the cornflour to a paste with the water. Add the mixture to the pan or wok. Cook, stirring, until the sauce thickens. Serve at once.

Nutrition Notes

Per portion:

Energy	118Kcals/493kJ
Protein	4.7g
Fat	3.8g
Saturated Fat	0.4g
Carbohydrate	15.9g
Fibre	1.3g
Sugar	9.3g
Sodium	0.67g

Spinach and Potato Galette

Creamy layers of potato, spinach and herbs make a warming supper dish.

Ingredients

Serves 6

900g/2lb large potatoes, scrubbed
450g/1lb fresh spinach
2 eggs
400g/14oz/1¾ cups low-fat cream
  cheese
15ml/1 tbsp grainy mustard
50g/2oz chopped fresh herbs (e.g.
  chives, parsley, chervil or sorrel)
salt and freshly ground black pepper

1 Preheat the oven to 180°C/ 350°F/Gas 4. Line a deep 23cm/ 9in cake tin with non-stick baking paper. Place the potatoes in a large pan and cover with cold water. Bring to the boil and cook for 10 minutes. Drain well and allow to cool slightly before slicing thinly.

2 Wash the spinach and place in a large pan with only the water that is clinging to the leaves. Cover and cook, stirring once, until the spinach has just wilted. Drain well in a sieve and squeeze out the excess moisture. Chop finely.

3 Beat the eggs with the cream cheese and mustard then stir in the chopped spinach and fresh herbs.

4 Place a layer of the sliced potatoes in the lined tin, arranging them in concentric circles. Top with a spoonful of the cream cheese mixture and spread out. Continue layering, seasoning with salt and pepper as you go, until all the potatoes and the cream cheese mixture are used up.

5 Cover the tin with a piece of foil and place in a roasting pan.

6 Fill the pan with enough boiling water to come halfway up the sides, and cook in the oven for 45–50 minutes. Turn out on to a plate and serve.

Nutrition Notes

Per portion:

Energy	230.83Kcals/972.16kJ
Protein	17.27g
Fat	5.98g
Saturated Fat	0.65g
Carbohydrate	28.57g
Fibre	3.77g
Sugar	3.58g
Sodium	4.38g

Braised Bean Curd with Mushrooms

The mushrooms flavour the bean curd beautifully to make this the perfect vegetarian main course.

INGREDIENTS

Serves 4
350g/12oz bean curd (tofu)
2.5ml/½ tsp sesame oil
10ml/2 tsp light soy sauce
15ml/1 tbsp vegetable oil
2 garlic cloves, finely chopped
2.5ml/½ tsp grated fresh root ginger
115g/4oz/1 cup fresh shiitake
 mushrooms, stalks removed
175g/6oz/1½ cups fresh oyster
 mushrooms
115g/4oz/1 cup drained, canned straw
 mushrooms
115g/4oz/1 cup button mushrooms,
 cut in half
15ml/1 tbsp dry sherry
15ml/1 tbsp dark soy sauce
90ml/6 tbsp vegetable stock
5ml/1 tsp cornflour
15ml/1 tbsp cold water
salt and ground white pepper
2 spring onions, shredded

1 Put the bean curd in a dish and sprinkle with the sesame oil, light soy sauce and a large pinch of pepper. Leave to marinate for 10 minutes, then drain the curd and cut into 2.5 x 1cm/1 x ½in pieces.

2 Heat the vegetable oil in a non-stick frying pan or wok. When it is very hot, fry the garlic and ginger for a few seconds. Add all the mushrooms and stir-fry for 2 minutes.

3 Stir in the sherry, dark soy sauce and stock, with salt, if needed, and pepper. Simmer for 4 minutes.

4 Mix the cornflour to a paste with the water. Stir the mixture into the wok and cook, stirring, until thickened.

5 Carefully add the pieces of bean curd, toss gently to coat thoroughly and simmer for 2 minutes.

6 Scatter the shredded spring onions over the top of the mixture, transfer to a serving dish and serve.

COOK'S TIP

If fresh shiitake mushrooms are not available, use dried Chinese mushrooms soaked in hot water.

NUTRITION NOTES

Per portion:	
Energy	122Kcals/510kJ
Protein	9.5g
Fat	7.4g
Saturated Fat	1.0g
Carbohydrate	3.6g
Fibre	1.2g
Sugar	0.3g
Sodium	0.63g

SALADS AND ACCOMPANIMENTS

Salads and vegetables as accompaniments play an essential part in healthy

eating. With the wonderful choice of vegetables available to us, and the

exciting ingredients introduced from around the world, we can enjoy

experimenting as well as eating healthily. Choose from Middle-eastern

Tabbouleh with Fennel and Pomegranate, crunchy stir-fried Spiced Vegetables

with Coconut, or warm Lentil and Cabbage Salad served with French bread,

to make satisfying side dishes at any time of the year.

Spiced Vegetables with Coconut

This spicy and substantial dish could also be served as a starter, or as a vegetarian main course for two. Eat it with spoons and forks, and chunks of granary bread for mopping up the delicious coconut milk.

INGREDIENTS

Serves 2–4 as a starter
1 red chilli
2 large carrots
6 stalks celery
1 bulb fennel
30ml/2 tbsp grapeseed oil
2.5cm/1in piece root ginger, peeled and grated
1 clove garlic, crushed
3 spring onions, sliced
400ml/14fl oz can thin coconut milk
15ml/1 tbsp fresh coriander, chopped
salt and freshly ground black pepper
coriander sprigs, to garnish

1 Halve, deseed and finely chop the chilli. If necessary, wear rubber gloves to protect your hands.

2 Slice the carrots on the diagonal. Slice the celery stalks on the diagonal. Trim the fennel head and slice roughly, using a sharp knife.

3 Heat the wok, then add the oil. When the oil is hot, add the ginger and garlic, chilli, carrots, celery, fennel and spring onions and stir-fry for 2 minutes.

4 Stir in the coconut milk with a large spoon and bring to the boil. Stir in the coriander and salt and pepper, and serve garnished with coriander sprigs.

---— COOK'S TIP —---

You can also eat these tasty spiced vegetables with noodles to create a more substantial dish.

--- NUTRITION NOTES ---

Per portion:
Energy	193Kcals/799kJ
Protein	2.9g
Fat	12.3g
Saturated Fat	1.6g
Carbohydrate	19g
Fibre	4.7g
Sugar	17.8g
Sodium	0.51g

Cracked Wheat and Mint Salad

Also known as bulgur wheat,
burghul or pourgouri, cracked
wheat has been partially cooked,
so it requires only a short soaking
before serving.

INGREDIENTS

Serves 4

250g/9oz/1⅔ cups cracked wheat
4 tomatoes
4 small courgettes, thinly sliced
4 spring onions, sliced on the diagonal
8 ready-to-eat dried apricots, chopped
40g/1½oz/¼ cup raisins
juice of 1 lemon
30ml/2 tbsp tomato juice
45ml/3 tbsp chopped fresh mint
1 garlic clove, crushed
salt and freshly ground black pepper
sprig of mint, to garnish

1 Put the cracked wheat into a large
bowl. Add enough cold water to
come 2.5cm/1in above the level of the
wheat. Leave to soak for 30 minutes,
then drain well and squeeze out any
excess water in a clean dish towel.

2 Meanwhile, plunge the tomatoes
into boiling water for 1 minute and
then into cold water. Slip off the skins.
Halve, remove the seeds and core and
roughly chop the flesh.

3 Stir the chopped tomatoes,
courgettes, spring onions, apricots
and raisins into the cracked wheat.

4 Put the lemon and tomato juice,
mint, garlic clove and seasoning
into a small bowl and whisk together
with a fork. Pour over the salad and
mix well. Chill in the refrigerator for
at least 1 hour. Serve garnished with a
sprig of mint.

NUTRITION NOTES	
Per portion:	
Energy	293Kcals/1231kJ
Protein	8.72g
Fat	1.69g
Saturated Fat	0.28g
Carbohydrate	62.64g
Fibre	2.25g
Sugar	0.24g
Sodium	0.09g

Lentil and Cabbage Salad

This warm crunchy salad makes a very satisfying meal if served with crusty French bread or wholemeal rolls.

INGREDIENTS

Serves 4–6

225g/8oz/1 cup puy lentils
1 garlic clove
1 bay leaf
1 small onion, peeled and studded with
    2 cloves
15ml/1 tbsp olive oil
1 red onion, finely sliced
2 garlic cloves, crushed
15ml/1 tbsp thyme leaves
350g/12oz cabbage, finely shredded
finely grated rind and juice of 1 lemon
15ml/1 tbsp raspberry vinegar
salt and freshly ground black pepper

1 Rinse the lentils in cold water and place in a pan with 1.3 litres/2¼ pints/6 cups cold water, peeled garlic clove, bay leaf and clove-studded onion. Bring to the boil and cook for 10 minutes. Reduce the heat, cover and simmer for 15–20 minutes. Drain; remove the onion, garlic and bay leaf.

——— NUTRITION NOTES———	
Per portion:	
Energy	240Kcals/1013kJ
Protein	16.5g
Fat	4.4g
Saturated Fat	0.4g
Carbohydrate	35.8g
Fibre	8.6g
Sugar	6.9g
Sodium	0.11g

2 Heat the oil in a large pan. Add the red onion, garlic and thyme and cook for 5 minutes until softened.

3 Add the shredded cabbage and cook for 3–5 minutes until just cooked but still crunchy.

4 Stir in the cooked lentils, lemon rind and juice and the raspberry vinegar. Season to taste and serve.

Tabbouleh with Fennel and Pomegranate

A fresh salad originating in the Middle East, with the added crunchiness of fennel and sweet pomegranate seeds. It is perfect for a summer lunch.

INGREDIENTS

Serves 6
225g/8oz/1 cup bulgur wheat
2 fennel bulbs
1 small fresh red chilli, seeded and
   finely chopped
1 celery stick, finely sliced
30ml/2 tbsp olive oil
finely grated rind and juice of 2 lemons
6–8 spring onions, chopped
90ml/6 tbsp chopped fresh mint
90ml/6 tbsp chopped fresh parsley
1 pomegranate, peel and pith removed
salt and freshly ground black pepper

1 Place the bulgur wheat in a bowl and pour over enough cold water to cover. Leave to stand for 30 minutes.

2 Drain the wheat through a sieve, pressing out any excess water.

3 Halve the fennel bulbs and cut into very fine slices.

4 Mix all the remaining ingredients together, including the soaked bulgur wheat and fennel. Season well, cover and set aside for 30 minutes before serving. Garnish with lettuce.

NUTRITION NOTES

Per portion:

Energy	209.66Kcals/876.5kJ
Protein	5.6g
Fat	6.12g
Saturated Fat	0.73g
Carbohydrate	34g
Fibre	2.26g
Sugar	4.48g
Sodium	0.01g

Marinated Cucumber Salad

Sprinkling the cucumber with salt draws out some of the water and makes them crisper.

INGREDIENTS

Serves 4–6
2 medium cucumbers
15ml/1 tbsp salt
90g/3½oz/½ cup granulated sugar
175ml/6fl oz/¾ cup dry cider
15ml/1 tbsp cider vinegar
45ml/3 tbsp chopped fresh dill
pinch of pepper

1 Slice the cucumbers thinly and place them in a colander, sprinkling salt between each layer. Put the colander over a bowl and leave to drain for 1 hour. Thoroughly rinse the cucumber under cold running water to remove excess salt, then pat dry on absorbent kitchen paper.

NUTRITION NOTES

Per portion:	
Energy	74Kcals/313kJ
Protein	0.4g
Fat	0.07g
Saturated Fat	0.0g
Carbohydrate	16.8g
Fibre	0.28g
Sugar	16.8g
Sodium	0.33g

2 Gently heat the sugar, cider and vinegar in a saucepan, until the sugar has dissolved. Remove from the heat and leave to cool. Put the cucumber slices in a bowl, pour over the cider mixture and leave to marinate for 2 hours.

3 Drain the cucumber and sprinkle with the chopped dill and pepper to taste. Mix well and transfer to a serving dish. Chill in the refrigerator until ready to serve. Garnish with a sprig of dill.

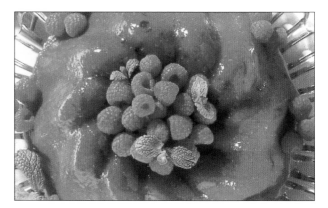

DESSERTS

There is no need to miss out on desserts when eating for a healthy heart.

All the delicious fruits that are so good for us can be transformed into

tempting desserts without the addition of high-fat ingredients. Nourishing

dried apricots combine with exotic fresh kumquats to make a spicy warm

dessert in Golden Ginger Compote. Frozen Apple and Blackberry Terrine,

and Passion Fruit and Apple Foam make a good choice when autumn fruits

are at their best. If you are entertaining, Minted Raspberry Bavarois or

Lemon Hearts with Strawberry Sauce will provide a sophisticated and

imaginative conclusion to a healthy dinner party.

Lemon Hearts with Strawberry Sauce

These elegant little hearts are light as air, and they are best made the day before your dinner party – which saves on last-minute panics as well!

INGREDIENTS

Serves 6
For the hearts
175g/6oz/¾ cup ricotta cheese
150ml/¼ pint/⅔ cup crème fraîche or
   soured cream
15ml/1 tbsp granulated sweetener
finely grated rind of ½ lemon
30ml/2 tbsp lemon juice
10ml/2 tsp powdered gelatine
2 egg whites
oil, for brushing

For the sauce
225g/8oz/2 cups fresh or frozen and
   thawed strawberries
15ml/1 tbsp lemon juice

1 Beat the ricotta cheese until smooth. Stir in the crème fraîche or soured cream, sweetener and lemon rind.

2 Place the lemon juice in a small bowl and sprinkle the gelatine over the top. Place the bowl over a pan of hot water and stir to dissolve the gelatine completely.

3 Quickly stir the gelatine into the cheese mixture, mixing it in evenly.

4 Beat the egg whites until they form soft peaks. Quickly fold them into the cheese mixture.

5 Spoon the mixture into six lightly oiled, individual heart-shaped moulds and chill the moulds until set.

6 Place most of the strawberries and the lemon juice in a blender and process until smooth. Pour the sauce on to serving plates and place the turned-out hearts on top. Decorate with slices of strawberry.

NUTRITION NOTES	
Per portion	
Energy	113.33Kcals/470.8kJ
Protein	6.15g
Fat	8.22g
Saturated Fat	5.14g
Carbohydrate	3.9g
Fibre	0.42g
Sugar	3.9g
Sodium	0.06g

Grilled Spiced Nectarines with Ricotta

This dessert is good at any time of the year – use canned peach halves if fresh ones are not available.

INGREDIENTS

Serves 4

4 ripe nectarines or peaches
15ml/1 tbsp light muscovado sugar
115g/4oz/½ cup ricotta cheese or
  low-fat fromage frais
2.5ml/½ tsp ground star anise

1 Cut the nectarines in half and remove the stones.

2 Arrange the nectarines, cut-side upwards, in a wide flameproof dish or on a baking sheet.

COOK'S TIP

Star anise has a warm, rich flavour – if you can't get it, try ground cloves instead.

NUTRITION NOTES

Per portion
Energy	136.25Kcals/577.2kJ
Protein	5.52g
Fat	3.36g
Saturated Fat	1.98g
Carbohydrate	22.49g
Fibre	2.4g
Sugar	22.49g
Sodium	0.03g

3 Stir the sugar into the ricotta or fromage frais. Using a teaspoon, spoon the mixture into the hollow of each nectarine half.

4 Sprinkle with the star anise. Place under a moderately hot grill for 6–8 minutes, or until the nectarines are hot and bubbling. Serve warm.

Minted Raspberry Bavarois

A sophisticated dessert that can be made a day in advance for a special dinner party.

INGREDIENTS

Serves 6

450g/1lb/2⅔ cups fresh or frozen and thawed raspberries
30ml/2 tbsp icing sugar
30ml/2 tbsp lemon juice
15ml/1 tbsp finely chopped fresh mint
30ml/2 tbsp/2 sachets powdered gelatine
75ml/5 tbsp boiling water
300ml/½ pint/1¼ cups custard, made with skimmed milk
250g/9oz/1⅛ cups Greek yogurt
fresh mint sprigs, to decorate

1 Reserve a few raspberries for decoration. Place the raspberries, icing sugar and lemon juice in a food processor or blender and process them until smooth.

NUTRITION NOTES	
Per portion	
Energy	144.16Kcals/611.66kJ
Protein	9.95g
Fat	4.08g
Saturated Fat	2.29g
Carbohydrate	18.13g
Fibre	1.88g
Sugar	15.35g
Sodium	8.98g

2 Press the purée through a sieve to remove the raspberry pips. Add the mint. You should have about 600ml/1 pint/2½ cups of purée. Sprinkle 5ml/1 tsp of the gelatine over 30ml/2 tbsp of the boiling water and stir until the gelatine has dissolved. Stir into 150ml/¼ pint/⅔ cup of the fruit purée.

3 Pour this jelly into a 1 litre/1¼ pint/4 cup mould, and leave the mould to chill in the refrigerator until the jelly is just on the point of setting. Tip the tin to swirl the setting jelly around the sides, and then leave to chill until the jelly has set completely.

4 Stir the remaining fruit purée into the custard and yogurt. Dissolve the rest of the gelatine in the remaining water and stir it in quickly.

5 Pour the raspberry custard into the mould and leave it to chill until it has set completely. To serve, dip the mould quickly into hot water and then turn it out and decorate it with the reserved raspberries and mint sprigs.

COOK'S TIP
You can make this dessert using frozen raspberries, which have a good colour and flavour. Allow them to thaw at room temperature, and use any juice in the jelly.

Golden Ginger Compote

Warm, spicy and full of sun-ripened ingredients – this is the perfect winter dessert.

INGREDIENTS

Serves 4

200g/7oz/2 cups kumquats
200g/7oz/1¼ cups dried apricots, soaked overnight in water
30ml/2 tbsp sultanas
400ml/14fl oz/1⅔ cups water
1 orange
2.5cm/1in piece fresh root ginger
4 cardamom pods
4 cloves
30ml/2 tbsp clear honey
15ml/1 tbsp flaked almonds, toasted

1 Wash the kumquats and, if they are large, cut them in half. Place them in a pan with the apricots, sultanas and water. Bring to the boil.

2 Pare the rind thinly from the orange and add to the pan. Peel and grate the ginger; lightly crush the cardamom pods and add to the pan with the cloves.

3 Reduce the heat, cover the pan and leave to simmer gently for about 30 minutes, or until the fruit is tender, stirring occasionally.

4 Squeeze the juice from the orange and add to the pan with honey to sweeten to taste. Serve warm and sprinkle with flaked almonds.

NUTRITION NOTES	
Per portion	
Energy	196.75Kcals/836kJ
Protein	4.57g
Fat	3.11g
Saturated Fat	0.23g
Carbohydrate	41.18g
Fibre	6.85g
Sugar	40.92g
Sodium	0.04g

Fresh Citrus Jelly

Fresh fruit jellies really are worth the effort – they're packed with fresh flavour, natural colour and vitamins – and they make a lovely fat-free dessert.

INGREDIENTS

Serves 4
3 medium-size oranges
1 lemon
1 lime
300ml/½ pint/1¼ cups water
75g/3oz/⅓ cup golden caster sugar
15ml/1 tbsp/1 sachet powdered
   gelatine
extra slices of fruit, to decorate

1 With a sharp knife, cut all the peel and white pith from one orange and carefully remove the segments. Arrange the segments in the base of a 900ml/1½ pint/3¾ cup mould or dish.

2 Remove some shreds of citrus rind with a zester and reserve them for the decoration. Grate all the remaining rind from the lemon and lime and one of the oranges. Place all the grated rind in a medium-size pan, with the water and sugar.

3 Heat gently until the sugar has dissolved, without boiling. Remove from the heat. Squeeze the juice from all the rest of the fruit and stir it into the pan.

4 Strain the hot liquid into a measuring jug to remove the rind (you should have about 600ml/1 pint/2½ cups: if necessary, make up the amount with water). Sprinkle the gelatine over the liquid and stir until it has completely dissolved.

5 Pour a little of the jelly over the orange segments and chill until set. Leave the remaining jelly at room temperature to cool, but do not allow it to set.

6 Pour the remaining cooled jelly into the dish and chill until set. To serve, turn out the jelly and decorate it with the reserved citrus rind shreds and slices of citrus fruit.

NUTRITION NOTES	
Per portion	
Energy	132.25Kcals/563.75kJ
Protein	4.56g
Fat	0.15g
Saturated Fat	0.01g
Carbohydrate	30g
Fibre	2.04g
Sugar	30g
Sodium	0.02g

Pears with Ginger and Star Anise

Star anise and ginger give a
refreshing twist to these poached
pears. Serve them chilled.

INGREDIENTS

Serves 4

75g/3oz/6 tbsp caster sugar
300ml/½ pint/1¼ cups white dessert
  wine
thinly pared rind and juice of 1 lemon
7.5cm/3in piece of fresh root ginger,
  bruised
5 star anise
10 cloves
600 ml/1 pint/2½ cups cold water
6 slightly unripe pears
25g/1oz/3 tbsp drained, preserved
  ginger in syrup, sliced
fromage frais, to serve

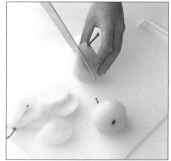

1 Place the caster sugar, dessert wine,
lemon rind and juice, fresh root
ginger, star anise, cloves and water into
a saucepan just large enough to hold
the pears snugly in an upright position.
Bring to the boil.

2 Meanwhile, peel the pears, leaving
the stems intact. Add them to the
wine mixture, making sure that they
are totally immersed in the liquid.

3 Return the wine mixture to the
boil, lower the heat, cover and
simmer for 15–20 minutes or until the
pears are tender. Lift out the pears with
a slotted spoon and place them in a
heatproof dish. Boil the wine syrup
rapidly until it is reduced by about half,
then pour over the pears. Allow them
to cool, then chill.

4 Cut the pears into thick slices and
arrange on four serving plates.
Remove the ginger from the wine
sauce, stir in the sliced, preserved
ginger and spoon the sauce over the
pears. Serve with the fromage frais.

NUTRITION NOTES	
Per portion:	
Energy	192Kcals/814kJ
Protein	0.5g
Fat	0.1g
Saturated Fat	0.0g
Carbohydrate	36.2g
Fibre	1.7g
Sugar	36.0g
Sodium	0.02g

Frozen Apple and Blackberry Terrine

Apples and blackberries are a classic autumn combination; they really complement each other. This pretty, three-layered terrine can be frozen, so you can enjoy it at any time of year.

Ingredients

Serves 6

500g/1¼lb cooking or eating apples
300ml/½ pint/1¼ cups sweet cider
15ml/1 tbsp clear honey
5ml/1 tsp vanilla essence
200g/7oz/2 cups fresh or frozen and
   thawed blackberries
15ml/1 tbsp/1 sachet powdered
   gelatine
2 egg whites
fresh apple slices and blackberries,
   to decorate

1 Peel, core and chop the apples and place them in a pan, with half the cider. Bring the cider to the boil, and then cover the pan and let the apples simmer gently until tender.

2 Tip the apples into a food processor and process them to a smooth purée. Stir in the honey and vanilla. Add half the blackberries to half the apple purée, and then process again until smooth. Sieve to remove the pips.

3 Heat the remaining cider until it is almost boiling, and then sprinkle the gelatine over and stir until the gelatine has completely dissolved. Add half the gelatine to the apple purée and half to the blackberry and apple purée.

4 Leave the purées to cool until almost set. Whisk the egg whites until they are stiff. Quickly fold them into the apple purée. Remove half the purée to another bowl. Stir the remaining whole blackberries into half the apple purée, and then tip this into a 1.75 litre/3 pint/7½ cup loaf tin, packing it down firmly.

5 Top with the blackberry and apple purée and spread it evenly. Finally, add a layer of the apple purée and smooth it. If necessary, freeze each layer until firm before adding the next.

6 Freeze until firm. To serve, allow to stand at room temperature for about 20 minutes to soften, and then serve in slices, decorated with fresh apple slices and blackberries.

Nutrition Notes

Per portion	
Energy	78Kcals/331.5kJ
Protein	3.63g
Fat	0.15g
Saturated Fat	0.0g
Carbohydrate	13.17g
Fibre	2.36g
Sugar	13.17g
Sodium	0.03g

Variation

For a quicker version the mixture can be set without the layering. Purée the apples and blackberries together, stir the dissolved gelatine and whisked egg whites into the mixture, turn the whole thing into the tin and leave the mixture to set.

Passion Fruit and Apple Foam

Passion fruit have an exotic, scented flavour that makes this simple apple dessert very special; if passion fruit are not available, use two finely chopped kiwi fruit instead.

INGREDIENTS

Serves 4
500g/1¼lb cooking apples
90ml/6 tbsp apple juice
3 passion fruit
3 egg whites
1 red-skinned apple, to decorate
lemon juice

1 Peel, core and roughly chop the cooking apples and place them in a pan, with the apple juice.

2 Bring to the boil, and then reduce the heat and cover the pan. Cook gently, stirring occasionally, until the apple is very tender.

3 Remove from the heat and beat the apple mixture with a wooden spoon until it becomes a fairly smooth purée (or purée the apple in a blender or food processor).

4 Cut the passion fruit in half and scoop out the flesh. Stir the flesh into the apple purée.

5 Place the egg whites in a clean, dry bowl and whisk them until they form soft peaks. Fold the egg whites into the apple mixture. Spoon the apple foam into four serving dishes.

6 Thinly slice the red-skinned apple and brush the slices with lemon juice, to prevent them from browning. Arrange the slices on top of the apple foam and serve cold.

— NUTRITION NOTES —	
Per portion	
Energy	74Kcals/318kJ
Protein	2.93g
Fat	0.21g
Saturated Fat	0.012g
Carbohydrate	16.27g
Fibre	2.75g
Sugar	16.27g
Sodium	0.05g

Angel Cake

Serve this light-as-air cake with low-fat fromage frais. It makes a perfect dessert.

INGREDIENTS

Serves 10

40g/1½oz/⅓ cup cornflour
40g/1½oz/⅓ cup plain flour
8 egg whites
225g/8oz/1 cup caster sugar, plus extra
  for sprinkling
5ml/1 tsp vanilla essence
icing sugar, for dusting

1 Preheat the oven to 180°C/350°F/Gas 4. Sift both flours on to a sheet of greaseproof paper.

— COOK'S TIP —

Make a lemony icing by mixing 175g/6oz/1½ cups icing sugar with 15–30ml/1–2 tbsp lemon juice. Drizzle the icing over the cake and decorate with physalis or lemon slices and mint sprigs.

2 Whisk the egg whites in a large grease-free bowl until very stiff, then gradually add the sugar and vanilla essence, whisking until the mixture is thick and glossy.

3 Gently fold in the flour mixture with a large metal spoon. Spoon into an ungreased 25cm/10in angel cake tin, smooth the surface and bake for about 45–50 minutes, until the cake springs back when lightly pressed.

4 Sprinkle a sheet of greaseproof paper with caster sugar and set an egg cup in the centre. Invert the cake tin over the paper, balancing it carefully on the egg cup. When cold, the cake will drop out of the tin. Transfer it to a plate, decorate if liked (see Cook's Tip), or dust with icing sugar and serve.

— NUTRITION NOTES —

Per portion
Energy	78Kcals/331.5kJ
Protein	3.63g
Fat	0.15g
Saturated Fat	0.0g
Carbohydrate	13.17g
Fibre	2.36g
Sugar	13.17g
Sodium	0.03g

Index

Mount Laurel Library
100 Walt Whitman Avenue
Mount Laurel, NJ 08054-9539
856-234-7319
www.mtlaurel.lib.nj.us